Investigating Health, Welfare and Poverty

Paul Trowler

Collins Educational

An imprint of HarperCollins*Publishers*

Second Edition published in 1996 by
Collins Educational
An imprint of HarperCollins*Publishers*
77–85 Fulham Palace Road
Hammersmith, London W6 8JB
First edition published in 1988 by Unwin Hyman Ltd

ISBN 0–00–322437–6

Paul Trowler asserts the moral right to be identified as the author of this work.
A catalogue record for this book is available from the British Library.

The author and publisher would like to thank the following people and organisations for permission to reproduce illustrations:
BBC Scotland (p.61); British Heart Foundation (p.83), Steve Bell (p.103); BUPA (p.112); Crisis (p.112); Format (pp.22, 70
(Ulrike Preuss), p.88 (Joanne O'Brien), p.121 (Brenda Prince), p.103 (Raissa Page)); Keith Gibson (p.30); Ronald Grant
(p.102); JAK, Associated Newspapers (p.1); Mary Evans Picture Library (pp.26, 50); Mencap (p.90); Photofusion (p.48
(Crispin Hughes), p.79 (Lawrence Gresswell), p. 96 (Gina Glover), p.137 (J. Southworth)); Rex Features (pp.115, 127, 138,
140); Virgin (p.67).
*While every effort has been made to contact copyright holders, the publisher would be pleased to hear from any copyright holder
who has not been acknowledged.*

Commissioned by Emma Dunlop
Edited by Susan Millership
Production by Mandy Inness
Cover artwork and design by Derek Lee
Illustrations by Julia Osorno
Cartoons by David Simonds
Typeset by Harper Phototypesetters Ltd, Northampton
Printed and bound by Scotprint Ltd, Musselburgh

Contents

Preface and How to Use This Book

This book uses a number of devices which may need explanation. They are:

Concept boxes: These define important ideas and, sometimes, theories at or near the location in the text where they are used.

Chapter bibliographies: This section, at the end of each chapter, gives the details of some of the key texts used in the chapter and helpful sources for further work on your own.

Tasks: Printed in italics and found throughout the book, these suggest activities which will enable individuals, pairs or groups of students to engage with the material discussed in the main text (see below for the rationale behind these).

Useful information/addresses: This section, at the end of chapters, gives the details of organisations and other information which may be able to help in your own investigations of health, welfare and poverty.

Examination questions: Past questions from the Associated Examining Board (which has the largest number of candidates in sociology at A level) are included at relevant points in the text. Try these on your own or with fellow students. Some skeleton answers are included at the end of the book for guidance. Common errors that students make are highlighted in the 'bad' outline answers. Use the 'good' outlines as a suggested basis to write your own answers (but remember that there are other ways of answering well).

The content of the book and the tasks around it put into practice a set of carefully researched educational principles based on findings from research on student learning. Authors such as N. Entwistle, P. Ramsden, R. Saljo, F. Marton and D. Laurillard are among those best known for this work, which was centred around universities in Sweden, Lancaster and Edinburgh. More recently the C.N.A.A.'s *Improving Student Learning Project* based at the Centre for Staff Development at Oxford Polytechnic has worked on clearly identifying and spreading good practice in teaching and learning based on that earlier work.

Essentially the research identified a number of different ways in which students went about the learning process. Some students were found to be effective learners in that their approach helped them develop a long lasting, structured and broad understanding of the material at hand and an ability to link it to other material. Other students adopted learning strategies which were less effective, resulting only in a relatively short-term memorising of facts in an unstructured and unconnected way. A number of 'learning pathologies' were also identified; traps into which the unwary student could fall. Among these are inappropriate use of 'operation learning' (learning in a serialist, stepwise way rather than a more holistic approach known as 'comprehension learning') and 'improvidence'; the failure to use common principles or to give sufficient detail in explanation.

Underlying all of this work are the concepts of deep and surface learning. Gibbs characterises the surface approach as follows:

'The student reduces what is to be learnt to the status of unconnected facts to be memorised. The learning task is to reproduce the subject matter at a latter date (e.g. in an exam).' (Gibbs, 1990, p3).

In taking a deep approach, on the other hand ...

'The student attempts to make sense of what is to be learnt, which consists of ideas and concepts. This involves thinking, seeking integration between components and between tasks, and 'playing' with ideas.' (Gibbs, 1990, p3).

The crucial point about the findings on students' different approaches to learning is that they are not fixed characteristics of the students themselves, rather they are strategies which tend to result from the organisation of the curriculum, of assessment techniques and of the way material is presented. In other words, individual students do not naturally or inevitably engage in poor (or good) learning strategies because of some basic feature they have as people. The same student may adopt surface approaches to learning in one subject and deep approaches to another. It is predominantly pedagogy, including the materials that support classroom practice, not psychology, that conditions learning strategy.

The content and tasks in this book, then, apply some of the principles identified by this research as facilitating a deep approach to learning. Those principles, as identified by the *Improving Student Learning Project*, are as follows:

1. Motivational context

'Deep learning is more likely when students' motivation is intrinsic and when the student experiences a need to know something. ... [they] learn best what they need to learn in order to carry out tasks which matter to them ...'

2. Learner activity

'Students need to be active rather than passive. Deep learning is associated with doing. If the learner is actively involved, then more connections will be made both with past learning and between new concepts. Doing is not sufficient for learning, however. Learning activity must be planned, reflected upon and processed, and related to abstract conceptions.'

3. Interaction with others

'It is often easier to negotiate meaning and to manipulate ideas with others than alone. The importance of discussion [or 'exploratory talk'] for learning is not a new idea ... and autonomous student groups and peer tutoring can be very effective ...'

4. A well structured knowledge base

'Without existing concepts it is impossible to make sense of new concepts. It is vital that students' existing knowledge and experience be brought to bear in learning. The subject matter being learnt must also be well structured and integrated...'. (Gibbs, 1990, p 9).

I hope that you enjoy using the book and find it helpful in achieving success.

Paul R. Trowler

Lancaster, 1996.

Reference

Gibbs, G. (1990) *Improving Student Learning Project Briefing Paper*, Oxford: Oxford Centre for Staff Development.

Social policy, health and welfare

Figure 1.1 The prescription charge finished him off!'

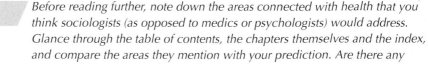

This chapter sets the scene for the rest of the book. In it we will examine some of the concepts used in the study of (in turn) health, welfare and poverty.

Health

Before reading further, note down the areas connected with health that you think sociologists (as opposed to medics or psychologists) would address. Glance through the table of contents, the chapters themselves and the index, and compare the areas they mention with your prediction. Are there any differences – extra areas or omissions?

The nature of 'health'

The World Health Organisation (WHO) defines health as:

'not the mere absence of disease, but total physical, mental and social well-being'.

Unfortunately this is so vague as to be almost useless. In practice the medical profession (and the population at large) tend to define health in a *negative* way, as:

'the condition in which there is an absence of disease or disability'.

This raises some problems too, mainly concerned with identifying when a disease is or is not present. The distinction between having a disease rather than just being 'off-colour', 'not on top form' and so forth is unclear.

The following process must occur before we are identifed officially as having a disease:

- recognition (of bodily events as symptoms of disease by the individual)
- definition (of the symptoms as serious enough to take to the doctor)
- action (specifically, of going to the doctor).

Only at this point is there an 'official' definition of ill-health, which may lead to further action such as hospitalisation, being prescribed a medicine or being given time off work. Doctors refer to the 'clinical iceberg' – that is, they only see those who present themselves to them and not the large proportion who are 'below the waves' and do not consult them.

Figure 1.2 The clinical iceberg

Table 1.1 gives the two-week incidence of symptoms and subsequent behaviour in a random sample of 1,000 adults living in London.

 Individually, brainstorm the factors that influence the decision to go to the doctor with an illness (include both 'pushing' and 'pulling' factors, that is, those

that impel you to go, and those that make you not want to).

In plenary, collate your ideas. What sociological insights does the resulting list give you about the clinical iceberg?

We cannot identify a 'normal' state, deviation from which counts as disease. This is because people's bodies are so different. In fact most of us put up with many symptoms for much of the time without ever going through the processes of recognition, definition and action. At any one time around 56 per cent of men and 70 per cent of women feel unwell in some way or have a recurring health problem. Yet men visit their doctor only three times a year, and women four times, on average.

Consequently, what counts as 'illness' differs between cultures and in history. What counts as 'health' must be socially constructed and is therefore variable too.

Some postmodernist sociologists have gone a long way towards claiming that health and illness are socially defined. Nigel Gilbert and Michael Mulkay (1984) have argued that the process of science, including medicine, has more to do with the social construction of understandings between scientists than with 'objective' knowledge.

Social constructionism

When we say something is 'socially constructed' (for example, ill-health) we mean that its important characteristics are defined by the attitudes, values and norms of behaviour that surround it in any given society or part of society, and that these actually shape the reality of that thing.

We should not, however, take the 'social constructionist' argument too far. Yanina Sheeran (1995) argues that some sociologists have taken this argument so far that:

they understate or devalue the real contributions Western medicine has made to health and the quality of life for many people;

they create a false opposition or binary divide between Western medicine and other approaches, when in fact they are complementary;

we have adopted an over-socialised conception of medicine. For example, it cannot seriously be that the WHO's claim to have eradicated smallpox is a social construction.

Table 1.1	
Individual with symptoms taking no action	188
Individuals with symptoms taking non-medical action	562
GP patients	168
Hospital out-patients	28
Hospital in-patients	5
Total (including 49 in sample with no symptoms – i.e. healthy)	1,000

Source: Wadsworth *et al.* (1971), quoted in Scrambler (1985), p. 43

She also argues that:

they are ideologically driven and make value judgements, often without acknowledging them explicitly;

comfortable Western sociologists can afford to be critical of Western medicine and 'relativise' health and illness, but the sick and starving in the Third World do not have that luxury.

From this point of view illness has a considerable objective reality which places limits on how far a sociological point of view can address it.

 Measures of the level of ill-health are available (infant mortality rate, expectation of life, etc.) but there is no measure of health. This has been an obstacle to the WHO's Health For All campaign – its success cannot be measured. Is it possible to develop a measure of health so that general improvements could be quantified at national level? If so, what form or forms might such a measure take?

The nature of 'disease'

Whereas 'illness' refers to the subjective feeling of 'not being well', the more specific term 'disease' refers to a medically diagnosed condition that has given rise to signs and symptoms in a patient. It is therefore possible to have no 'illness', yet have a disease. An example of this is someone with symptomless ('asymptomatic') high blood pressure ('hypertension'). They are not ill, but they have a disease.

 Give an example of the reverse – someone who is ill, but does not have a 'disease'.

Table 1.2 lists the 17 categories of diseases identified by the WHO.

 In which category would the following diseases go:

AIDS, schizophrenia, asthma, stomach cancer, stomach ulcers?

Doctors are concerned to establish the aetiology of a disease, that is, its causes. This can best be done through large-scale epidemiological studies of its incidence. For example, the link between cigarette smoking and lung cancer was discovered in the following way:

• Doctors noticed that among lung-cancer patients smokers outnumbered non-smokers.

• A survey was carried out among lung-cancer sufferers and this confirmed the correlation between smoking and the disease (though this did not necessarily mean smoking caused it, merely that the two were often found together).

• Finally, work in the laboratory demonstrated that elements in cigarettes could cause cancer in animals, and the mechanism by which this occurred was identified.

Other terms commonly used in the study of disease are *morbidity* and *mortality*. Morbidity refers to ill-health resulting from disease, mortality to death. The mortality rate is the number of deaths in a given year and place per 1,000 of the population.

Examination question

'Health and illness must be seen as conditions which are both socially caused and socially defined.' Examine the evidence for this view.

AEB AS Paper 2, Summer 1994, question 5

A skeleton answer for this question is on p. 146.

Table 1.2 Diseases identified by the WHO

Category of disease	Examples
1. Infections and parasitic diseases	Malaria, viral hepatitis
2. Neoplasms	Hodgkin's disease, malignant neoplasm of the larynx
3. Endocrine, nutritional and metabolic diseases and immunity disorders	Diabetes mellitus, gout
4. Diseases of blood and blood-forming organs	Iron-deficiency anaemia, diseases of white blood cells
5. Mental disorders	Alcohol-dependence syndrome, physical symptoms of mental disorder
6. Diseases of the nervous system and sense organ	Epilepsy, migraine
7. Diseases of the circulatory system	Hypertension, acute myocardial infarction
8. Diseases of the respiratory system	Asbestosis, acute sinusitis
9. Diseases of the digestive system	Appendicitis
10. Diseases of the genitourinary system	Renal failure, female infertility
11. Complications of childbirth and pregnancy	Excessive vomiting in pregnancy
12. Diseases of the skin and subcutaneous tissue	Dermatitis, psoriasis
13. Diseases of the musculoskeletal system and connective tissue	Rheumatoid arthritis
14. Congenital anomalies	Spina bifida, cleft palate
15. Certain conditions originating in the perinatal period (i.e. just prior to and soon after birth)	Slow foetal growth, birth trauma
16. Symptoms, signs and ill-defined conditions	Symptoms involving head and neck, sudden death – cause unknown
17. Injury and poisoning	Fracture of carpal bone, poisoning by psychotropic drugs

Source: World Health Organisation (1977) *International Classification of Diseases*, 9th edn, Geneva: WHO

> Choose any of the individuals named in Table 1.3 and research their contribution
> to the development of medicine. (Note: table continues on next page.)

Table 1.3 Some important developments in medicine

Years	Eras	Individuals	Events and trends
10,000 BC 3,000 BC	Prehistoric	None that we know about	Belief in magic – charms, spells, etc. Primitive surgery – trepanning. Use of plants, roots and berries as medicines. Ideas about medicine limited by supernatural view of world. Problem for historians of no written evidence.
	Egyptian	Imhotep	*Egyptians* – superstition mixed with a more scientific approach. Use of drugs and preservatives – embalming. Very aware of hygiene – washed frequently. Settled way of life helped ideas to develop and they were written down. Religious beliefs stopped them using dissection, so they knew little about how the body worked.
	Chinese	Asclepios Hippocrates	*Greeks* – strong supernatural beliefs but believed in hygiene and fitness. Philosophers and doctors studied the human body at Alexandria where dissection was permitted.
	Indian		
	Greek		*China* – discoveries made here long before Europe.
400 AD	Babylonian		Use of acupuncture. *India* – skilled surgeons. *Babylon* – one of the first cities to have public health facilities.

Years	Eras	Individuals	Events and trends
400 AD	Roman	Galen	Importance of public health – sewers, drains, aqueducts and public baths. Military hospitals. Spread of Empire meant spread of ideas. Large number of unqualified doctors meant that most were distrusted.
1500 AD	Dark Ages and Middle Ages	Avicenna Rhazes Albicasis	Little progress in medicine in Europe due to fall of Roman Empire and influence of Church which believed that disease was a punishment from God. Black Death. Arab Empire – centre of medicine. Growth of medical schools – Salerno and Cairo.
1700 AD	Renaissance	Vesalius Pare Harvey Paracelsus Sydenham	Increase in books and travel encourages spread of ideas. Study of anatomy becomes more common. Much greater awareness of causes of disease and way the body works.
1900 AD	18th and 19th Centuries	Jenner Pasteur Simpson Lister Semmelweis Nightingale Koch Chadwick Freud	Industrial Revolution – growth of towns leads to overcrowding. Public Health Acts in Britain (1848 and 1875) passed to improve sanitation and prevent the spread of disease. Growth of hospitals. Improvements in nursing. Rapid progress in all areas of medicine in 19th century – understanding of germs, use of chloroform in surgery, vaccination, etc.
2000 AD	20th Century	Ehrlich Manson Fleming Barnard	Much greater understanding of disease and its treatment including syphilis, TB, diptheria and malaria. National Health Service and growth of Welfare State in Britain. World wars lead to improvements in drugs, surgery and the fight against disease. World Health Organisation – spread of health education and prevention of disease in Third World. Use of high technology in Western hospitals.

Source: L. Hartley, *The History of Medicine*, Basil Blackwell

The NHS today

The National Health Service cost in the region of £39 billion a year to run in 1994–5. In recent years it has been the subject of considerable criticism and subsequent reorganisation.

From 1948 to 1974 responsibility for the nation's health was shared by:

- regional hospital boards (hospitals),

- authorities (ambulance and home health support services, etc.), and

- local executive councils (GPs and other services).

This tripartite structure caused considerable administrative headaches and was criticised for being a particularly expensive form of management. The costs of the NHS had risen, instead of falling as Beveridge believed they would as the health of the population improved as a result of its work.

In 1974 the NHS was reorganised so that the vast majority of its services came under the control of (in order of diminishing size) regional health authorities, area health authorities and local district management teams. A new complaints procedure was set up. In each district there was (and still is) a community health council (CHC), which monitors the running of the district's health services and receives complaints from the public. CHCs have been criticised for being ineffective and composed mainly of middle-class members who are out of touch with the health problems of ordinary people. Another means of complaint about health services is the NHS Ombudsman, also established in 1974. Once again, the limited powers of this office mean that there is little faith in its effectiveness.

The telephone number and address of your local CHC is in the phone book. They will be happy to tell you about their work (this is part of their function).

1 *Find as much information about them as you can and make a presentation to the group you are studying with.*

2 *You can conduct a similar exercise for the NHS Ombudsman. The address to write to if you are in England is:*
The Health Service Commissioner for England,
Church House,
Great Smith Street,
London SW1P 3BW

3 *One measure of the effectiveness of policies for the redress of grievances is the number of people in the population who are aware of their existence and how to call upon their services. Develop a means of quantifying this.*

Before long the new structure, too, was felt to be inefficient and ineffective. In 1983 the area health authorities had been abolished, and their functions were allocated to reorganised district health authorities. The structure of the NHS today is outlined in Figure 1.3.

On 31 January 1989 the Government announced what Health Secretary Kenneth Clarke referred to as 'the most formidable programme of reform in the history of the NHS'. The discussion document, a White Paper called *Working For Patients* (Cmnd 555) made the following proposals:

Many hospitals should become self-governing and should sell services to doctors, health authorities, private patients and other hospitals. They would be given resources by the NHS, though these would reflect the ability of hospitals to attract patients.

Many doctors should be given more financial responsibility by being given their own funds to administer and targets of cost-effectiveness to be met (failure to do so would result in financial penalties). Costs of prescribed drugs, for example, would be carefully monitored in each practice. Again, funds from the NHS would be related to the doctor's 'attractiveness' to patients. Doctors would be allowed to advertise.

District health authorities should become more like agencies – not providing health services but buying them for patients from hospitals and doctors. Management at all levels of the NHS (regional health authorities, district health authorities, family

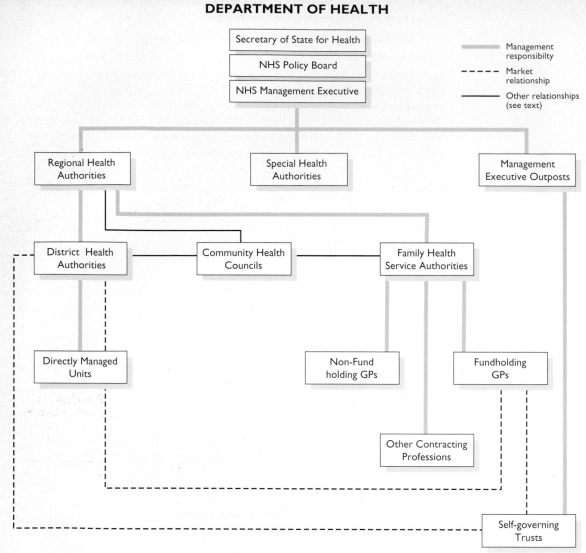

DEPARTMENT OF HEALTH

Secretary of State for Health

NHS Policy Board

NHS Management Executive

Management responsibilty

Market relationship

Other relationships (see text)

Regional Health Authorities

Special Health Authorities

Management Executive Outposts

District Health Authorities

Community Health Councils

Family Health Service Authorities

Directly Managed Units

Non-Fund holding GPs

Fundholding GPs

Other Contracting Professions

Self-governing Trusts

Figure 1.3 The National Health Service

Source: Baggott (1994)

practitioner committees) would become more like that of businesses, with a general manager and finance director. Local authorities and health professionals would lose much of their representation on these bodies.

Cost-effectiveness throughout the system would be carefully monitored by auditors (accountants), and all parts of the service (including the previously powerful consultants) would be answerable to management for lack of efficiency or effectiveness.

The NHS and Community Care Act 1990 (which came into effect in 1991) was the result. It allowed hospitals to opt out of district health authority control while remaining NHS hospitals. In April 1991 fifty-seven hospital trusts were formed, and there have been three more waves of opting out since then. A distinction between 'purchasers' and 'providers' has been introduced, and health authorities have a new role as purchasers of health services for the populations in their districts. GPs can elect to become fundholders, exercise more control over their budgets and 'shop around' for the services their patients needed.

Thus an 'internal market' was created within the health service. Table 1.4 and Figure 1.4 illustrate how it works.

Table 1.4 The 'internal market' within the health service	
Strategic decision makers and central funding	Secretary of State and Department of Health Regional health authorities Family Health Service Associations
Purchasers	District health authorities Fundholding GPs
Providers	Hospitals (directly managed units) Hospitals (Trusts) GPs (fundholding and non-fundholding)

Source: Taylor and Field (1993)

Figure 1.4

Source: Taylor and Field (1993)

Sellers/providers

Community health services (District nurses etc)

Purchasers/ commissioners

District Health Authorities

NHS Hospital Trusts

+ Private pay beds

+ subcontracted sevices In private sector – 'hotel' and catering, private ambulance services etc

Purchasers/ commissioners

Fund-holding GPs

NHS Hospitals – directly managed units

+ Private pay beds

Other trusts (ambulance services etc)

These developments should not be seen in isolation. They mirror very closely government policy in other fields under its direct control. Christopher Pollitt (1993) considers these sorts of initiatives as part of a general system which he calls 'managerialism'. According to Pollitt, managerialism is:

> 'a set of beliefs and practices, at the core of which burns the seldom tested assumption that better management will prove an effective solvent for a wide range of economic and social ills'.

Managerialism stresses increased productivity through stringent control of the production process by managers who are given the power to manage. The three Es are paramount: economy, efficiency and effectiveness. In practical terms it gives rise to the following sorts of activities:

activity costing

devolved budgeting to 'line managers'

performance indicators that stress economy and efficiency (not effectiveness)

staff appraisal schemes

merit pay

objective setting

considerable rhetorical emphasis on responsiveness to the consumer

principals and heads of department who have become 'managers' and 'directors', increasingly removed from 'clients' (e.g. patients).

Pollitt argues that managerialism is a kind of second best for New Right policy makers. What they would prefer is complete privatisation of the public services. However, this would be politically unacceptable (the British electorate would reject the idea of wholesale privatisation of the Welfare State) and would be very difficult practically:

> 'The only remaining political option, therefore, is to improve the *productivity* of these services so that their quality can be maintained or even increased while the total resourced devoted to them is held down.'

The Labour Party, though, has claimed that Conservative government policies on the NHS have been paving the way for privatisation. By restricting services they have also effectively been forcing people to turn to the private sector to ensure they get good-quality treatment within a reasonable timescale.

Pollitt has been one among many academic critics of managerialism. Some of the most important criticisms have been the following:

It relies on an over-simple model of motivation. It assumes that people are motivated to work harder by the prospect of increased financial reward – a form of Taylorism. Taylorism has been demonstrated to be only a partial view of human motivation. It is certainly a highly inappropriate model of motivation for workers in the Welfare State and the public services generally.

Taylorism

Based on the work of Frederick ('Speedy') Taylor in the USA during the early part of this century, Taylorism is a management theory that advocates the careful analysis of tasks within a process to find the most efficient method of completing them. Workers should be carefully selected and given financial incentives to work as efficiently as possible. Time and motion study and Ford's car assembly methods are based on Taylorism.

It relies too heavily on management information systems. It assumes that with the right hardware and software top management can have information about, and control, all aspects of the operation. This has increasingly proved to be untrue. Workers on the ground have to be given decision-making latitude in any case.

It lacks an understanding of the multiple and conflicting goals and loyalties of staff. Staff working in the NHS are often highly committed to patient care, over and above loyalty to the specific organisation they are working in. Failing to understand this leads to demoralisation in the workforce and associated problems.

It mistakenly applies the ethics of entrepreneurialism to the public services. The whole idea of injecting market principles into health and other services is inappropriate. For example, the entrepreneur makes profits through exploiting clients' ignorance of other traders and has an interest in keeping them ignorant. The profit motive may take precedence over successful outcomes.

It raises equal opportunities concerns. Managerialism creates a workaholic, 'macho' ethos that comes to permeate organisations exposed to it. This leads to the exclusion of those who have domestic responsibilities. Many posts now cause stress, and long working hours are written into the job description. Rather than seeing more women moving into management with a greater variety of possible management styles and role models, we are witnessing a creeping 'hard' managerialism in the public sector that associates managerial competency with masculinity.

Welfare

A Welfare State can be defined as:

> 'a state with a democratic form of government which assumes responsibility for the well-being of its citizens through a range of interventions in the market economy'.

The term includes both the idea of state responsibility for the welfare of its citizens and the institutions and practices through which this idea is realised. By 'market economy' we mean an economy in which enterprise is in private hands and which operates on the basis of the search for profit. Market economies are contrasted to command economies, where the state controls (and usually owns) the means of production.

There is a common misconception that the Welfare State in Britain came into existence in the 1945–51 period of post-war Labour government. In fact, as Table 1.5 on p. 13 shows, its history is much longer than that. However, the structure of the modern Welfare State and many of the principles operating today were established then, following the recommendations of the Report on National Insurance and Allied Services of 1942, chaired by Lord Beveridge. Beveridge identified 'five giants' which it was the duty of the state to tackle and eliminate. They were:

- idleness (unemployment)

- disease (poor health)

- ignorance (lack of education)

- squalor (poor housing)

- want (poverty).

 Beveridge concentrated on these five areas for social policy in his report. Which of the following additional areas of government intervention do you think should be considered part of the Welfare State?

- *Services for old people (e.g. old people's homes)*
- *Tax relief for mortgages and dependants ('fiscal social security')*
- *Refuse collection*
- *Services for gypsies and vagrants*
- *Personal social services (social work)*
- *Environmental protection*
- *Employment services*
- *Planning services*
- *Probation and after-care services for offenders*
- *Services for children and young people*
- *Transport services (roads, buses, rail)*
- *Leisure services (leisure centres, swimming pools)*
- *Job perks: free membership of BUPA, pension, car, etc. ('occupational social security'), which are partly funded by the state through tax relief.*

The state and welfare in Britain

 Identify three commercial organisations involved in the provision of welfare services.

There are three ways in which the state can be involved in welfare. These are:

1 provision of services directly (e.g. benefits from the DSS)

2 subsidy of services (An important example here is the Training Commission, later to become TEED, funding voluntary organisations – giving £285 million to Community Programme schemes in 1983/4.)

3 regulation of services (e.g. legislation on rented housing).

Table 1.5 summarises the history of the Welfare State in Britain as far as the statutory sector is concerned.

 Choose any one of the reports or Acts of Parliament referred to in this time chart and research it. Use the references listed in the bibliography to help you. Report back to the group you are studying with when you have finished.

However, the state is only one of the providers of welfare services. The Wolfenden Report (*The Future of Voluntary Organisations,* 1978) identified four sectors that can provide social services and health care:

1 statutory (organisations set up by legislation in Parliament)

2 voluntary (non-statutory organisations, often charities)

3 commercial (profit-making businesses)

4 informal (relatives, neighbours and friends).

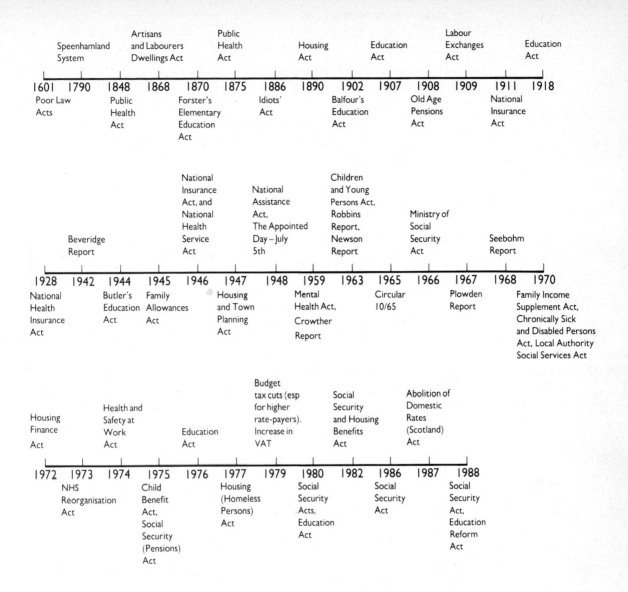

Table 1.5 The history of Britain's Welfare State

Individually, compile a list of all the voluntary welfare organisations you can recall. In plenary, collate your lists. Choose any one and, in pairs, research its history and current work. Identify which organisations are active in your area. Addresses can be found in The Charities Digest and from the Volunteer Centre (see bibliography and useful information).

In Britain welfare is provided by a combination of these four sectors, a situation which the Wolfenden Report called 'welfare pluralism'. The Conservative governments since 1979 have attempted to alter the mix of this pluralism, reducing the traditionally strong role of the state and increasing the role of the other three sectors. Their reasons for this are, in summary, based on the following beliefs:

State organisations are 'captured' by professionals who use them in their own interests, not for their clients.

State services are expensive and bureaucratic compared to other forms of provision. Private schemes and charitable agencies provide more choice and efficiency than state schemes.

State organisations are too large and unresponsive to the needs and wishes of clients, and as a result people no longer support them.

Generally, state intervention in society should be reduced so that people become more responsible for themselves and their families (a reduction of the role of the 'nanny state' and its attendant 'dependency culture', to use Mrs Thatcher's terms).

Compulsory insurance, state programmes, etc., belong to the pre-war and early post-war eras; they are out of date in modern society.

The strategy of equality (i.e. redistributing resources from the rich to the poor through welfare benefits and services) has gone far enough — probably too far.

The costs of the Welfare State are too great: demand is unlimited, and there are constantly rising expectations.

Government action has unintended consequences — e.g. the importance of the family declines, people become unwilling to work for low wages, incentives to succeed are reduced.

Government has become overloaded: the system is too complex and outcomes are no longer predictable.

Government spending on welfare is counter-productive: it creates inflation, which only causes further problems.

Governments act according to the 'vote motive', that is, they offer welfare goodies as a bribe for election or re-election. This means that welfare services are set up irresponsibly, without thought to cost or consequences.

1 *What are the particular advantages of (a) commercial, (b) voluntary, and (c) informal provision of services?*

2 *The following are the possible different relationships between the four sectors of welfare provision. Under each one, give an example of a service that falls within this category in Britain and the sector or sectors that provide it (for example, under 'Sole provider' would come social clubs for the elderly or handicapped provided by voluntary organisations such as Help the Aged).*

Sole provider   Temporary relief Complementary   Competitive

Funding the Welfare State

The NHS in particular has been plagued by questions of funding — how much should be spent on it, and how far patients should be asked to contribute to expenses (for example, through prescription charges and 'hotel bills' for stays in hospital). Similar sorts of questions have surrounded the issue of welfare benefits — how generous they should be, how 'scroungers' should be rooted out, whether such benefits should go only to the most needy, and so on.

Questions like these became particularly important as the British economy went into

Figure 1.5

decline in the early 1970s. Though, arguably, the economy has now recovered, funding is still at the root of a crisis in the Welfare State. There are several aspects to this crisis:

The government's desire to cut public expenditure means that Welfare State spending is seen as a barrier to recovery and prosperity.

The government's desire to cut taxes means that there are inadequate funds for health and welfare services.

There has been a loss of public confidence in the idea of the Welfare State, which has affected attitudes to it, both inside and outside its institutions.

Demographic factors have not helped: an increasingly ageing population places greater financial burdens on the health and social services.

Medical treatment is becoming more expensive as it increasingly involves high technology and expensive drugs. It therefore demands an ever higher proportion of state expenditure.

As medical expertise becomes greater and the potential for curative medicine improves, demand increases. If access to medical services is easy and free or cheap there is potentially unlimited demand (particularly in view of the flexible way in which 'ill-health' is defined and the changing definitions of 'normal health'). Left alone, the medical profession would want to increase the resources available to it to meet this demand. There would be a spiral in expenditure which would lead to severe economic problems nationally. The government's responsibility, therefore, is to limit the responsibilities of the Welfare State.

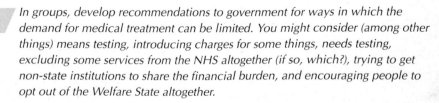

In groups, develop recommendations to government for ways in which the demand for medical treatment can be limited. You might consider (among other things) means testing, introducing charges for some things, needs testing, excluding some services from the NHS altogether (if so, which?), trying to get non-state institutions to share the financial burden, and encouraging people to opt out of the Welfare State altogether.

Successive Conservative governments have maintained that the Welfare State is safe in their hands, and indeed that funding for it has increased since Labour left office in 1979. However, these contentions are matters of considerable debate.

Poverty

Chapter 4 will discuss the problems associated with defining 'poverty'; here we will concentrate on examining the changing attitudes towards poverty in Britain.

The earliest official responses to poverty began with the Poor Law Acts of the early seventeenth century. Parishes (and after 1782 'unions' – combinations of parishes) provided relief for orphans, the sick and the aged. Workhouses were run for the able-bodied poor. Some of these were privately run (receiving a fee from the parishes for the poor they accepted), and conditions in them were very bad. In these early days the attitude towards the poor was that if they were able-bodied 'sturdy beggars' their poverty was the result of indolence or some other personal failing.

In 1795 there was the beginning of a change in this attitude. Some of those in positions of power began to appreciate that poverty could be caused by inadequate wages and unemployment resulting from factors over which the individual worker had no control. A system of poor relief known as the Speenhamland System was introduced in that year in Berkshire and quickly spread around central and southern England. It gave a supplement to wages to workers who had large families and whose income was inadequate. It was also 'index linked' in that the amount of income supplement given depended upon the price of bread at the time.

Of the numerous problems connected to the Speenhamland System the one that most exercised the minds of those in power was its cost. The 'poor rate' (the tax collected to pay for relief of the poor) increased dramatically with its introduction. It was primarily this that led to the Poor Law Amendment Act of 1834. This marked a return to the view that poverty was the fault of the poor themselves, who (unless they were orphans, sick or old) should be punished. The able-bodied poor were no longer eligible for 'outdoor relief' and had to enter workhouses. These were deliberately kept as unpleasant as possible in accordance with the principle of 'less eligibility' – the idea that conditions should be as bad as possible to make entering a workhouse less attractive than even the worst kind of employment outside. This had the desired result: many people declined to accept 'indoor relief'. In times of unemployment this had the effect of creating much poverty and misery. The authorities, however, believed it was forcing the idle to work.

The Poor Law of 1834 continued to operate virtually unchanged until 1908. Then there was another swing in attitudes towards the poor, partly in response to studies of poverty conducted by Charles Booth and Seebohm Rowntree (see pages 48–50). Again it was realised that involuntary unemployment and low wages could cause poverty just as much as sickness and old age and that poverty was an economic problem, not a moral one. A new set of legislative measures was introduced, gradually replacing the old Poor Law. Old age pensions were introduced (for some) in 1908, and limited health and unemployment insurance was set up by the government in 1911. These were the precursors of the modern Welfare State.

It can be argued that during the 1980s there was a revival of attitudes similar to those that inspired the 1834 Poor Law Amendment Act. The view that the principal cause of poverty is the ignorance and idleness of the poor themselves seems to have become dominant once again, at least in some quarters. The new tough mood was encapsulated in legislation. The Social Security Act of 1986 (which came into operation in 1988) has been called the most important social welfare measure since the post-war legislation that followed the Beveridge Report. It introduced the following measures:

It replaced Supplementary Benefit with Income Support (both being non-contributory and means-tested). As a result the level of benefit for many (particularly the young) was reduced, benefit was cut entirely in some cases (for example, for young people who moved away from their families without good reason), and discretionary payments for cases of special hardship were eliminated.

It set up the Social Fund, partly to help those cases of special hardship now not covered by Income Support. However:

- almost all payments are loans, not (as before) grants;

- they do not have to be paid – the Government can decide;

- there is only a limited amount in the Social Fund each year;

- claimants in a financial crisis must look elsewhere for money first;

- appeals will not be to independent bodies but to the Department of Social Security (DSS).

It replaced Family Income Supplement with Family Credit, which in some ways is more generous but may not be claimed by many of those eligible for it (family heads in work but on low incomes).

It reduced the amount of state pension for those retiring early next century by limiting the link between earnings now and pension then. At the same time the Act made it easier and cheaper to take out private pensions (though with these there is no guarantee what the eventual pension will be).

Other legislative measures concerning poverty have consolidated this new approach. The 1988 Social Security Act withdrew benefits from most people under 18. Its assumption was that young people should either be in jobs or accept a place on the Youth Training Scheme. One official of the Trades Union Congress said of this measure: 'We are heading for a new Dickensian era where instead of little match girls we have drug addicts and child prostitutes' (quoted in the *Independent,* 28 December 1988, p. 4). It was estimated that at least 14,000 people between the ages of 16 and 17 were without jobs or income during Christmas 1988.

Other Conservative social security measures of recent years include the following. Explain them in terms of the New Right philosophy (outlined on pages 24–26).

Child Benefit was not increased in line with inflation in some years (child benefit is a universal benefit which is paid to all mothers with more than one child).
Prescription charges were progressively increased (from 20p in 1979) and charges were introduced for dental checks and eye tests.
After 1982 local education authorities were not obliged to provide school meals (except for some benefit claimants) or nursery education.
The council house building programme was halted or cut in a number of years.
Income tax was reduced dramatically between 1979 and 1988, most of the benefit going to higher-rate taxpayers (the maximum rate was cut to 60%).
Domestic rates were abolished and replaced by the Poll Tax. The level of rates paid increased the more land you owned and the bigger and better your

house, but the Poll Tax was a flat-rate charge on individuals, regardless of the
property the owned.

People between the ages of 16 and 18 were denied income support (in all but
exceptional circumstances), a Youth Training place being officially available
for all (Social Security Act 1988).

Resources for the DSS to identify fraudulent claimants were greatly increased.

The effect of the social security changes was to leave 80 per cent of the poorest
claimants worse off than they were before April 1988 and to intensify the poverty
trap. A study of 30,000 people who consulted the Citizens Advice Bureaux in May
1988 was conducted by that organisation. Its main findings were that:

stricter means tests meant higher rates of non-claiming;

some claimants who took a job found themselves worse off as the amount of work
people could do and still claim Income Support was cut from 30 hours to 24 hours;

people in work and claiming Family Credit were frequently worse off because their
mortgage interest payments were no longer made for them;

single parents in work and claiming benefit found their child care and work expense
payments cut;

grants for tools and clothing to help people start work were no longer available;

benefits were no longer payable during the first two weeks of work;

cuts in housing benefit left the majority worse off;

compensation for the loss of free school meals was inadequate, again leaving
claimants worse off.

Essay

'What counts as illness and health differs both historically and geographically.'
Explain this statement and discuss the problems it poses both for sociologists
and for medics.

'The purpose of Newspeak was not only to provide a medium of
expression for the world-view and mental habits proper to the
[inhabitants of that country] . . . but to make all other modes of
thought impossible. It was intended that . . . a heretical thought . . .
should be literally unthinkable . . . Its vocabulary was so constructed
as to give exact and often very subtle expression to every meaning
that a Party member could properly wish to express, while excluding
all other meanings . . .' – George Orwell, *Nineteen Eighty-Four*

Terms generated by government in the field of social welfare often seem to have the
characteristics of Newspeak. 'Community care' is a good example: the word
'community' suggests a warm, strong and cooperative group, and 'care' also evokes
very positive associations. In the past the terms used in welfare policy were not so
carefully constructed. The following are some examples of now outmoded terms:

National Assistance
Family Allowance

Rent and rate rebates
Labour Exchange.

Compile a list of modern welfare policy terms (particularly the names of types of social security benefits) and comment on their connotations.

Bibliography

Alcock, P. (1987) *Poverty and State Support,* London: Longman

Allsop, J. (1984) *Health Policy and the NHS,* London: Longman

Baggott, R. (1994) *Health and Health Care in Britain,* New York: St Martin's Press

Barker, P. (ed.) (1984) *The Founders of the Welfare State,* London: Heinemann

Baugh, W. E. (1987) *Introduction to the Social Services,* London: Macmillan

Beveridge, W. (1942) *Social Insurance and Allied Services,* Cmd 6404, London: HMSO; reprinted 1984

Brenton, M. (1985) *The Voluntary Sector in British Social Services,* London: Longman

Brenton, M. and Ungerson, C. (annually) *The Yearbook of Social Policy,* London: Longman

Charities Digest, published annually by the Family Welfare Association

Committee of Inquiry into the Future Development of the Public Health Function Public Health in England, London: HMSO (1988)

Gilbert, N. and Mulkay, M. (1984) *Opening Pandora's Box,* Cambridge: Cambridge University Press

Graham, H. (1985) *Health and Welfare,* London: Macmillan

Ham, C. (1985) *Health Policy in Britain,* 2nd edn, London: Macmillan

Hartley, L. (1988) *The History of Medicine,* Oxford: Blackwell

Johnson, N. (1987) *The Welfare State in Transition,* Hemel Hempstead: Wheatsheaf

—— (1990) *Reconstructing the Welfare State,* Hemel Hempstead: Wheatsheaf

Mishra, R. (1984) *The Welfare State in Crisis,* Brighton: Wheatsheaf

Papadakis, E. and Taylor-Gooby, P. (1987) *The Private Provision of Public Welfare,* Brighton: Wheatsheaf

Pollitt, C. (1993) *Managerialism and the Public Services,* 2nd edn, Oxford: Blackwell

Scrambler, G. (1985) 'Illness behaviour', in M. Morgan *et al., Sociological Approaches to Health and Medicine,* London: Croom Helm

Sheeran, Y. (1995) 'Sociology, biology and health', *Sociology Review,* Vol. 4, No. 4

Taylor, S. and Field, D. (1993) *Sociology of Health and Health Care,* Oxford: Blackwell Science

Thane, P. (1982) *The Foundations of the Welfare State,* London: Longman

Watkin, B. (1975) *Documents on Health and Social Services - 1834 to the Present Day,* London: Methuen

Wadsworth *et al.* (1971) *Health and Sickness,* London: Tavistock

Wolfenden, J. (1978) *The Future of Voluntary Organisations,* London: Croom Helm

World Health Organisation (annual) *World Health Statistics,* London: HMSO

Useful information

The Volunteer Centre is the national advisory agency on volunteer and community involvement. Its address is 29 Lower Kings Road, Berkhamsted, Herts, HP4 2AB (Tel: 014427 73311).

A useful publication on statutory and non-statutory organisations, legislation, etc., concerning health, welfare and poverty is the *Social Services Yearbook,* published annually by Pitman.

2 Perspectives on health, welfare and poverty

Figure 2.1 'And how many patients do you lose in this sort of operation, Doctor?'

This chapter examines some of the important perspectives on the issues of health, welfare and poverty. These are phenomenology, interactionism, the New Right, the Social Democrats, functionalism, Marxism, feminism and postmodernism. You should read the chapter in conjunction with Chapter 3 so that you can make links between perspectives and methods of research.

The phenomenological perspective

From a phenomenological perspective the first thing to do when researching issues of health, welfare and poverty is to dispense with preconceptions. Events must be treated as 'strange' – the researcher should refuse to participate in the shared meanings that underlie all social interaction. Doing this enables him or her to uncover the nature of those meanings (which are normally so obvious to the participants that they are not conscious of their presence). The researcher, then, behaves like a

Martian seeing human interaction for the first time – s/he is free of any of the influences of socialisation.

The phenomenological perspective in sociology argues that:

the social world has no objective existence: its reality is nothing more than the shared meanings and beliefs we have about it;

these meanings seem so obvious to the members of a society that they do not notice them – they take them for granted;

the task of the sociologist is to uncover these meanings, not in an attempt to establish any scientific laws or universal truths about social behaviour but to show how particular small social systems work.

For example, what is 'common sense' to an Australian aborigine is completely alien to a British person, and vice versa. The two are living in completely different worlds. These worlds have been and are being constructed for them and by them in the course of their social interaction. While this may be clearly true in the aborigine/British example, it is also true for closer cultures (such as France and Italy) and for groups within one culture (civil servants in London and young unemployed in Glasgow).

Anthropologists (students of 'simple' societies) use this sort of method in their studies. They usually come from cultures which are radically different from the ones they are studying, so for them the phenomenological perspective is relatively easy to adopt. However, their training and experience make them good at using 'ethnomethodology' (as this approach is called) in their own cultures too. An example of its use in the study of health comes from a book called *Medical Encounters*. Its editors say:

> 'We asked our contributors to treat their own experiences [of illness and health care] as "strange" and to prepare an account of how they attempted to produce order out of these experiences . . .' (Davis and Horobin 1977, p. 10)

For one of the contributors, anthropologist Rosemary Firth, who was admitted to a tropical diseases hospital after fieldwork in Malaysia, the experience was an excellent opportunity to observe the NHS as she would a tribe in the Far East:

> '. . . at 4.00 p.m. nurses in white uniforms (?lowest grade) came round with trolleys . . . At 8.15 p.m. hot drinks were brought round. When we were all safely in bed, a nurse (white uniform, no belt buckle) looked in to ask if anyone wanted a sleeping tablet . . . After tea at 6.00 a.m., and breakfast in bed about 7.30 a.m., a flock of activities and routines to be noted. Pulse, temperature, weighing, blood samples taken, instructions about preserving specimens given; a series of people in different coloured overalls bring in instruments for cleaning – dusting, polishing and so on. Green overalls bring food and clean. Pink overalls seem to take away the pans and dusters.' (*Ibid.*, pp. 114–15)

Figure 2.2 A consultation
with the doctor

Write a similar account of a consultation you have had with a GP. Pay special attention to the symbols of office, the stages of the consultation, who spoke when, what was said, etc. Remember to treat every stage as 'strange'. Use the photograph above to help you.

You should note the following points about 'applied' phenomenology:

Only small-scale studies are done (e.g. one ward in a hospital).

No 'laws' or general statements about social behaviour are made, only descriptions of behaviour and suggestions about the underlying commonsense ideas of the participants.

The researcher must make great effort at every moment of the study not to take anything for granted.

1 Why are the studies small scale, and why do they not produce any 'laws' of social behaviour?
2 What other areas concerned with health, welfare and poverty might be suitable for this sort of study?
3 Are there any ways in which this approach could be useful to social policy makers?
4 Have you any general criticisms of the phenomenological perspective and ethnomethodology?

Interactionism

Interactionism concentrates on interpersonal behaviour in small groups, particularly on the effects the attitudes and beliefs held by one person or group can have on others' behaviour and perceptions. It is based on the following assumptions:

• Perception of ourselves and others is based on symbols or labels (e.g. I am shy, you are moody and unpredictable, she is intelligent and knowledgeable, he is unreliable, they are stupid, lazy and prone to crime).

- These labels are not necessarily based on fact.

- However, they influence our behaviour and that of others.

- Actions based on them can make the image become reality.

- Equally, people may reject labels, dispel them and create new ones.

Thus the labels or images we have of other people and groups (and of ourselves) are in a constant state of flux, of negotiation and renegotiation. Some are more durable than others, some are only partial. When we meet someone new we have the elements of a label ready for them (because of the way they speak and look, the clothes they are wearing, the way they behave and so on). We merely need to fill in the details. All of these things will be influenced by that person's self-perception and the image they are trying to create. Having fixed an idea of 'what this person is like', we behave towards them in a particular way, and this will influence the way they behave with us. Meanwhile, of course, the other person is doing the same things with regard to us. We do not even have to meet people for this process to occur – images are formed about black people, football supporters and drug takers, for example, from all sorts of sources. These images may influence our behaviour in many ways.

In what areas of the fields of health, welfare and poverty are these insights relevant?

In *Worlds Apart: Professionals and Their Clients in the Welfare State* Tim Robinson (1978) notes how the symbols of the medical profession are used by doctors to control their encounters with their patients. This starts from the moment a patient enters the room:

> 'She is faced by a white-coated doctor, often behind his desk, sometimes surrounded by some of the esoteric symbols of his profession. He may well also have a deferential bevy of medical students, an odd nurse and maybe a visitor or two . . . In that situation the consultant clearly controls the whole encounter. Everyone waits on his questions, actions and movements. Frequently he will ask questions of the [patient] with little explanation of their relevance and will make little attempt to explain what he makes of the answers. Taken *in toto* a very powerful message of the importance . . . and strange expertise of the doctor is spelt out and the [patient] who feels sufficiently at home, confident and significant to take an active part in what is going on is probably the exception.'

Other sociologists have noted the consequences for various groups of this sort of interaction. Ann Cartwright and Mary O'Brien (1978) found that the working class receive inferior treatment from the medical profession because they are labelled as uneducated and unlikely to understand explanations about their illness or proposed treatments, so they are rarely given such explanations (see page 8). Erving Goffman (1961) documented the consequences of interactions in mental institutions (page 106), and Hilary Graham and Ann Oakley (1981) showed how pregnancy and childbirth are perceived in very different ways by doctors and mothers, with the doctor's approach prevailing (see page 99).

1 In what ways could policy makers implement the insights offered by this
   perspective?
2 Are studies based on an interactionist perspective necessarily small scale like
   those of phenomenology?
3 What criticisms have you of the interactionist perspective?

The New Right

Figure 2.3 Michael Portillo,
a leading member of the
New Right

New Right thinking has informed government policy since 1979 when the
Conservatives were elected to power. Although some people consider New Right
ideology and Thatcherism to be the same thing, Mrs Thatcher's ideology represented
only one aspect of the New Right, as we will see.

The fundamental ideas behind new right thinking can be summed up in these key
points:

Market forces raise standards; organisations (e.g. hospitals) and individuals (e.g.
   doctors) who have to fight for success in a competitive environment either
   improve or go under.

Freedom for the consumer (the patient or client) is central; if they are free to make
   decisions in a crowded market, the market is truly competitive. Interference in
   their choices by government or anyone else is counterproductive.

State intervention restricts individual freedom; people need to be left to make their
   own decisions. When state bureaucracies become involved they start operating in
   their own interests and against those of the people.

Information is crucial for consumers to be able to make choices; without information
   on which to base choices the market is not really free.

Individual rather than collective freedoms should be encouraged; individuals,
   especially enterprising individuals, are crucial to the future of the nation. In fact,

according to Mrs Thatcher, 'there is no such thing as society, only individuals and families'.

These are neo-liberal ideas: they stress *freedoms* (hence the word 'liberal', as in 'liberate'). However, the neo-conservative element of the New Right stresses constraint and the need for the state to intervene in the market. Neo-conservatives distrust individuals and believe that they need to be watched and controlled. Thus the government is concerned not to give too much power to doctors and hospital trusts. It restricts their power by keeping a tight grip on the purse strings. William Kickert (1991) refers to this as 'steering at a distance'. Andrew Gamble (1988) argues that the two strands within New Right philosophy are in tension, leading to unworkable and contradictory social policies.

The specific arguments that the New Right make against the Welfare State are summarised on pp. 13–14. They do not suggest that the Welfare State should be abolished, however, merely that welfare policy should be in line with the 'residual model', which holds that those who need state help form a small group at the bottom of society (see Figure 2.4). Benefits should be targeted at them (and only them) and should be minimal. Universal provision of benefits is nonsensical; it gives to those who do not need it and wastes resources. Child Benefit, for example, cost over £5 billion a year in 1992, going to nearly 7 million households with 12 million children, regardless of income.

Figure 2.4 The vertical and static nature of the residual model

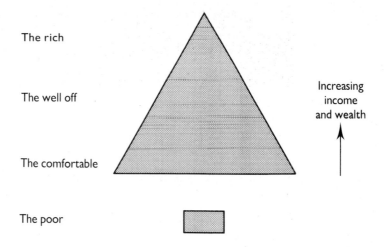

The rich

The well off

The comfortable

The poor

Increasing income and wealth

The residual model of poverty relies on the ability of the caring agencies to identify those in need. This is done primarily through means testing. Means-tested welfare is cheap, efficient and effective. Its effectiveness is a double one in that, being cheap, taxes can be reduced and the incentive to work is increased as a result. This will increase the prosperity of the country in the long term. Means testing also limits the demand for goods and services. For example, charging for eye tests and dental check-ups (which were free until 1989) cuts down on unnecessary demand for these services.

> *What arguments are there against means testing and in favour of universal benefits?*

The 1986 Social Security Act, summarised on page 16, reflected the Conservatives' New Right philosophy in the following ways:

It emphasised the family (for example, by denying benefit to young people who leave their families without a job).

It attempted to promote self-reliance and independence (for example, by encouraging people to provide their own pensions and by making people pay back money from the Social Fund).

In line with the residual model of welfare, it provided support only to the worst off (for example, by making the Social Fund available only as a last resort).

> 1 *What five policies would take priority if you headed a newly elected government with a strong New Right philosophy?*
> 2 *What criticisms do you have of the New Right perspective?*

Examination question

> *'The provision of universal welfare benefits is responsible for the continued existence of poverty.' Evaluate the arguments for and against this viewpoint.*
>
> AEB A-level, November 1993, Paper 2, question 6

Social Democrats

Figure 2.5 Sir William Beveridge, architect of the Welfare State

Social Democrats base their views on the twin pillars of John Maynard Keynes and Lord Beveridge. Keynes provided the economic theory, Beveridge the social component of their thought.

Keynes argued that the government could manage demand for goods and employment levels in the economy through careful intervention, notably by varying its own spending and taxing policies. Beveridge argued in favour of compulsory insurance for each member of society to protect them against the hazards of a market economy. Everybody should be insured and everybody should be eligible to receive state benefits.

This 'institutional model' of welfare (see Figure 2.6) contrasts strongly with the New Right's residual model, which, in the eyes of Social Democrats, leads to social division and the marginalisation of the poor and needy. Beveridge believed that it was the duty of the individuals in society to stand together, the strong supporting the weak. Though for some it may mean that the costs of welfare outweigh the benefits they receive, at least they have the satisfaction of contributing to the general good and knowing that if they should fall on hard times they too will be supported by the community.

The advantages of a unified system of social insurance over separate policies administered by private companies were claimed by Beveridge to be:

• convenience – only one authority to deal with;

Figure 2.6 The horizontal and dynamic nature of the institutional model

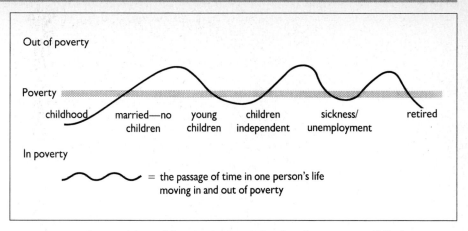

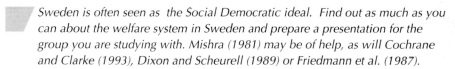

- no demarcation problems (disputes between bodies about responsibility);

- no gaps in cover;

- absolute security of benefit;

- uniform rates and conditions;

- uniformity of procedure;

- economies in administrative costs through concentration of administration in one body.

> *Sweden is often seen as the Social Democratic ideal. Find out as much as you can about the welfare system in Sweden and prepare a presentation for the group you are studying with. Mishra (1981) may be of help, as will Cochrane and Clarke (1993), Dixon and Scheurell (1989) or Friedmann et al. (1987).*

Functionalism

Functionalism is a sociological perspective that sees in social organisation many similarities to the physical make-up of an animal's body. Both the body and society consist of distinguishable parts (legs, eyes, etc., for the one, the church, family, etc., for the other). In both animals and society the parts all play some clear role – they fulfil a function (movement, vision, social integration, human reproduction and so forth). In both, too, the different parts act together to form a system which (usually) operates smoothly to fulfil the goals of the whole. The functionalists maintain, then, that:

- societies are made up of social institutions (the parts);

- these parts perform identifiable functions; and

- together the parts make up the social system (the interacting whole).

> *List three social institutions other than the church and the family. What functions do they perform for society?*

At least in its early days (at the end of the last century and the first half of this one) functionalism tended to see everything in society as fulfilling some sort of function. As in animals, there was no room for dead weight – anything that was not of use was eliminated by natural selection.

Functionalism as applied to the study of health, welfare and poverty makes the following assertions:

Poverty is functional for society: it motivates people to take menial jobs, creates jobs in the 'caring' professions, makes those who are not suffering poverty feel good, provides incentives for social mobility, and so on.

However, those marginalised by excessive poverty may cause social upheaval by civil unrest, even revolution.

Therefore the institutions of the Welfare State are necessary to integrate the poor into society by limiting the deprivation they suffer. Both poverty (at a certain level) and the Welfare State (appropriately developed) are useful to society.

The functionalist view of ill health was elaborated by one of the best-known functionalists, Talcott Parsons. He studied psychology in the early part of his career, and perhaps as a result he concluded that most ill health was psychosomatic (the result of psychological rather than physical factors). He held that becoming ill is often the result of a conscious or unconscious *decision* on the part of the person concerned, usually because his or her normal role obligations in society have become too demanding. For instance, people often fall ill or suffer accidents because they have chosen to expose themselves to infection or risk. Minor ailments may be imagined to be serious and may even become so because of the patient's response. Mental illness can also be the result of such choices.

By becoming 'ill' the patient is escaping into a sick role. This has four main aspects, according to Parsons (see Table 2.1):

The sick person is exempt from certain social responsibilities.

S/he cannot be expected to take care of himself or herself, or to get rid of the illness by 'willpower'.

S/he should want to get well.

S/he should seek medical advice and cooperate with medical experts.

The sick role is functional in that it prevents the formation of a subculture of the sick. Such a subculture would be disruptive to the social system as it would develop a set of norms and values that legitimated incapacity, fatalism, dependency, non-work and so on. The sick role prevents this happening by ensuring that the sick person interacts with doctors, friends and relatives, rather than other sick people. The sick role also denies legitimacy to being sick because of the third and fourth points outlined above. Thus it helps avoid the situation in which a significant part of the population becomes sick in order to avoid work and other social responsibilities.

To sum up, then, the functionalist position on health, welfare and poverty is as follows:

- The institutions and characteristics associated with these issues (the Welfare State, poverty, the sick role) are functional in that they keep society integrated and working properly.

Table 2.1 Parsons' analysis of the roles of patients and doctors

Patient: sick role	Doctor: professional role
Obligations and Privileges	*Expected to*
1. Must want to get well as quickly as possible.	1. Apply a high degree of skill and knowledge to the problems of illness.
2. Should seek professional medical advice and cooperate with the doctor.	2. Act for welfare of patient and community rather than for their own interest, desire for money, advancement, etc
3. Allowed (and may be expected) to shed some normal activities and responsibilities (e.g. employment, household tasks).	3. Be objective and emotionally detached (i.e. should not judge patients' behaviour in terms of personal value system or become emotionally involved with them.)
4. Regarded as being in need of care and unable to get better by his or her own decision and will.	4. Be guided by rules of professional practice.
	Rights
	1. Granted right to examine patients physically and to enquire into intimate areas of physical and personal life.
	2. Granted considerable autonomy in professional practice.
	3. Occupies position of authority in relation to the patient.

Source: Patrick and Scrambler (1986)

- However, it is important that the levels of poverty, ill health and so on are neither too high nor too low.

- Thus the welfare aspects of the social system need to constantly monitor and adapt to the changing levels of these phenomena to ensure balance (a process of 'homoeostasis' – stability through movement).

> 1 *In what ways could policy makers implement the insights offered by this perspective?*
> 2 *Are studies based on a functionalist perspective likely to be small scale or large scale? Why?*
> 3 *What criticisms have you of the functionalist perspective?*

Functionalism differs from Marxism, which we will examine next, in that while functionalists see society as based on agreement and operating in the interests of all, Marxists see it as based on exploitation and conflict. However, there are similarities: both see the demands of the whole social system as conditioning the development of welfare institutions within it. Both see individuals as relatively unimportant; they are merely part of larger social institutions (the economic system, classes). Both see these institutions as operating in a functional manner, though for Marxists the functions are being performed for the benefit of only a few people in society rather than for everyone.

Marxism

Figure 2.7 Preparing the next generation of the proletariat?

According to Marxists, all societies that have existed so far have been divided into two (or sometimes more) social classes which have directly competing interests. Under Britain's capitalist system the workers – who are trying to sell their labour for the highest price – are in direct competition and sometimes conflict with the capitalists – who are trying to cut costs and maximise profits by paying the lowest possible wages.

The main elements of the Marxist view of the Welfare State are these:

The Welfare State was created to pacify the workers by giving them a stake in society and (through the discipline imposed by the educational system) training them to be obedient to their employers.

The Welfare State actually benefits the capitalists most because it provides them with a healthy, well-housed, state-subsidised and well-educated workforce and a reserve army of unemployed labour maintained by the state, ready to work if required.

The costs of welfare are borne not by the capitalists but by the state, which pays for it with money raised through a taxation system. The tax burden falls most heavily on those who can least afford it.

The Welfare State was never designed to eradicate poverty or reduce social inequality: its main principle is merely to ensure that no one starves, thereby reducing the chances of a violent revolution.

The rich benefit from the Welfare State not only because it provides them with a suitable workforce but it also gives them benefits through the tax system (relief on mortgages, company cars and expense accounts, etc.) as well as direct benefits (such as free or subsidised schooling, higher education, health care, transport and so on).

Some Marxists take a rather more positive view of the Welfare State. For example, for Ian Gough (1979) the growth of social expenditure in the 1960s and 1970s was the product of working-class pressure on the state. As there was full employment unions could use the threat of strikes to push for more concessions from both employers and the state. Indeed, Karl Marx himself believed that welfare measures implemented in the nineteenth century had been introduced under pressure of working-class action.

Marxists have a distinctive view of biomedicine (for a definition of this term, see Chapter 8) as well as the Welfare State. For them capitalist medicine is used as a means of social control, manipulating behaviour to keep it within the bounds of the 'normal'. Some of the ways this is done are:

alleviating the symptoms caused by an unhealthy capitalist system, thereby making the system more bearable (treating the headache, not the noisy working conditions that caused it);

legitimating official attempts to change people's behaviour by deeming that behaviour to be both unhealthy and indulged in only by weak or stupid people (advising against promiscuity, illegal drug use, etc.);

acting as a gate-keeper, ensuring that only those who are 'acceptably sick' are allowed to have time away from work with pay.

There are many similarities between the apparently opposed perspectives of the New Right, particularly its neo-liberal wing, and Marxism. They agree that everyone wants the government to spend more but do not want higher taxes. They agree that there is government overload, so that its job is not done effectively and there are insufficient resources. They agree that welfare benefits and services often go to people who do not need them.

There are similarities, too, with functionalism. Marxists like James O'Connor are really arguing that the Welfare State is functional for the capitalist economic and social system. The functionalists would not disagree with this (though they would use different terms). Some contemporary Marxists have, however, moved away from this 'functionalist Marxism', particularly in seeking to show the contradictions between a capitalist state and a Welfare State – especially the 'fiscal crisis' or what André Gunder-Frank (1980) calls 'welfare farewell'.

 1 Has Marxism anything useful to say to policy makers?
2 What criticisms have you of the Marxist perspective?

Feminism

Feminists consider that the welfare system incorporates the patriarchal (male-dominated) ideology found in the rest of society. Examples to illustrate this are numerous; some of the best known are as follows:

The insurance system that existed between the two world wars largely excluded married women, who were considered to be the responsibility of their husbands.

The family household system is a miniature welfare system that relies on the unpaid and unrecognised work of women.

Until the European Court ruled the distinction discriminatory in the mid-1980s, married women could not claim Attendance Allowance for looking after a disabled relative (since caring was their responsibility anyway, the thinking ran), though men (married or single) and single women could.

Women are expected to lift the burden of welfare from the state by looking after elderly and sick relatives, especially with the advent of 'community care' (see page 121).

Women bear the brunt of poor housing and low levels of benefit as men assign them the responsibility for staying at home, feeding the family and so on.

Until very recently married women's income tax affairs had to be handled by their husbands so that the woman was legally obliged to disclose all her financial information to the man, but not vice versa.

The education system has traditionally given restricted access to females, and continues to serve them badly.

As far as poverty is concerned, a disproportionate number of the poor are women. This is because:

women tend to be found in low-paid, part-time and insecure jobs;

women live longer and therefore comprise the majority of the elderly poor;

since women are deemed responsible for childcare, they are likely to have gaps in payments into pension funds and National Insurance, resulting in lower benefits on retirement

Women's health is discussed extensively in Chapter 6. Here we need merely note that women generally suffer worse physical and mental health than men.

The root causes of this situation are interpreted differently by different schools of feminism. For Marxist feminists these disadvantages result from women's role in servicing the capitalist system. By bearing and caring for children they reproduce the proletariat for capitalists, at the same time as keeping the current generation well-fed, housed and happy – and all this at no cost to the capitalists. The family household system is the principal method by which this is achieved, so Marxist feminists want to abolish this system as well as fundamentally changing the economic system.

Radical feminists identify men in general rather than the male capitalists in particular as responsible for women's oppression. For many of them the answer lies in withdrawal from and opposition to the patriarchal society and its welfare institutions. Women's self-help groups, hospitals and clinics for women only, women's cooperatives and so on offer the best chance for escaping from patriarchal oppression.

For the more 'moderate' liberal feminists there is nothing immutable about the current situation. Reform is possible, and women can implement changes by capturing positions of power. Public opinion can be changed through the media and through pressure group activity. Sexist laws can be repealed (as in the examples of Attendance Allowance and income tax law mentioned above), and progressive new legislation (such as the Sex Discrimination Act) can be brought in.

Feminists identify a number of problems in the fields of health, welfare and poverty.

   1 In groups, describe six social changes you would recommend to put these problems right. In a plenary session, compare your lists.

   2 What criticisms have you of the feminist perspective?

Postmodernism

Bryan Turner (1993) suggests that a postmodern model of science, including medical science, will consist of at least the following propositions:

There is no longer a single coherent rationality; rather there are competing notions of what is rational. We live in a fragmented, diversified and decentralised world; there are many ways of understanding our world and many ways of expressing our understandings ('discursive forms').

The 'grand narratives' of previous eras, including science, have now collapsed due to the demise of our faith in a single rationality. We have instead a pile of competing myths and stories.

The hierarchies within science and other fields have broken down. There is now very little to distinguish between elite culture and popular or mass culture. One flows into the other; individuals access both.

The role of the intellectual has changed, partly because of the merging of elite and popular culture. The intellectual (for example, the medical researcher) is as likely to appear on popular television as at an academic conference. This is an aspect of the marketisation and consumerism which are typical of postmodern society.

The distinctions between types of judgement (for example, aesthetic and moral) have become blurred as a result of all of the above. Similarly it becomes difficult for the individual to distinguish between the 'fictional' and the 'real'. The two merge into a kind of 'hyper-reality' (Baudrillard, 1985).

All of this means that the traditional status of those involved in health and welfare, such as health professionals, has evaporated. They are just another part of the specific type of consumer society that is postmodernity. People may equally well turn to alternative therapies, organised religions, cults or any other of the many competing 'solutions' to the problems they may have. Similarly, medical science and the particular set of understandings that medicine propounds have become just another competing 'story' among the multitude. Zigmund Bauman (1988) sums up this point of view as follows:

> 'It was the intellectuals who impressed upon the once incredulous population the need for education and the value of information. Here as well their success turns into their downfall. The market is only too eager to satisfy the need and supply the value. With the DIY (electronic) technology to offer, the market will reap the rich crop of the popular belief that education is a human duty and (any) education is useful.'

 Ernest Gellner (1992) has written a strident critique of postmodernism. One of the things he says is that that there are no postmodernists at 30,000 feet.

1 *What do you think he means by this, and how may the comment apply to the postmodernists' account of medical science? (You may find it helpful to refer back to Chapter 1 and the criticisms of the social construction of health/ill health thesis summarised by Yanina Sheeran – page 3).*

2 *If you are studying as a class, divide yourselves into seven small groups and each one select one of the perspectives outlined above (Phenomenological, Interactionism, The New Right, Social Democrats, Functionalism, Marxism, Feminism and Postmodernism). Prepare to conduct a discussion on one of the following issues:*

The future of the NHS
The role of the family in health, welfare and poverty
The causes of poverty

Document A

A state which does for its citizens what they can do for themselves is an evil state ... In such an irresponsible society no one cares, no one saves, no one bothers – why should they when the state spends all its energies taking money from the energetic, successful and thrifty to give to the idle, the failures and the feckless?

Document B

After trial of a different principle, it has been found to accord best with the sentiments of the British people that in insurance organised by the community by use of compulsory powers each individual should stand in on the same terms; none should claim to pay less because he is healthier or has more regular employment. In accord with that view, the proposals of the report mark another step forward to the development of State insurance as a new type of human institution, differing both from the former methods of preventing or alleviating distress and from voluntary insurance. The term 'social insurance' to describe this institution implies both that it is compulsory and that men stand together with their fellows. The term implies a pooling of risks ...

1 *Identify which perspective these two quotes come from. Give reasons for your answer.*
2 *Choose one other perspective on health, welfare and poverty and show how an adherent of this perspective would react to the ideas expressed in documents A and B.*
3 *Though these have all been called 'perspectives' it may be more precise to*

say that some are political ideologies while others are sociological perspectives. Listed below are the characteristic features of both of these. After reading about each perspective, and using any other knowledge you may have about it, tick the appropriate boxes under the statements. *(The boxes represent the perspectives, with the initial above each.)*

Sociological perspective		Political ideology

1. Describes how society works   OR   Makes judgements about the 'good' society

P   I   NR   SD   FNC   M   FMNSM   PM   P   I   NR   SD   FNC   M   FMNSM   PM
☐ ☐ ☐ ☐ ☐ ☐ ☐ ☐   ☐ ☐ ☐ ☐ ☐ ☐ ☐ ☐

2. Is interested in all facets of the operation of society   OR   Tends to concentrate on certain parts of society's operation, particularly on how resources are (or should be) distributed to individuals and groups within society

P   I   NR   SD   FNC   M   FMNSM   PM   P   I   NR   SD   FNC   M   FMNSM   PM
☐ ☐ ☐ ☐ ☐ ☐ ☐ ☐   ☐ ☐ ☐ ☐ ☐ ☐ ☐ ☐

3. Is based on a well-developed theory   OR   Is based on values

P   I   NR   SD   FNC   M   FMNSM   PM   P   I   NR   SD   FNC   M   FMNSM   PM
☐ ☐ ☐ ☐ ☐ ☐ ☐ ☐   ☐ ☐ ☐ ☐ ☐ ☐ ☐ ☐

4. Has a body of knowledge, based on research, to support it.   OR   Uses any available evidence that supports its case

P   I   NR   SD   FNC   M   FMNSM   PM   P   I   NR   SD   FNC   M   FMNSM   PM
☐ ☐ ☐ ☐ ☐ ☐ ☐ ☐   ☐ ☐ ☐ ☐ ☐ ☐ ☐ ☐

5. Suggests strategies for the successful study of society   OR   Suggests policies for the improvement of society

P   I   NR   SD   FNC   M   FMNSM   PM   P   I   NR   SD   FNC   M   FMNSM   PM
☐ ☐ ☐ ☐ ☐ ☐ ☐ ☐   ☐ ☐ ☐ ☐ ☐ ☐ ☐ ☐

4a Construct a matrix with eight sections along the vertical axis (one for each of the perspectives we have examined) and eight along the horizontal axis. This gives sixty-four boxes. Along the top of the matrix put the following questions, in turn, above each section:

Does it focus on interpersonal behaviour?
Does it take a national perspective?
Does it favour major change in the welfare system?
Does the Welfare State significantly alter the social structure?
Does it prefer a quantitative or qualitative methodology?
Who benefits most from the Welfare State?
Who loses most from the Welfare State?
Are there any 'baddies'?

4b Now taking one perspective each (alone or in small groups), complete the boxes.

5a Which perspectives do the following statements illustrate?

'The state can do most for the poor by encouraging them to help themselves.'
'United action to change the institutions which make them poor is the only long-term solution to poverty. It must be done by the poor themselves.'
'The state has a responsibility for the sick, poor and helpless.'

5b Write three similar statements to illustrate different perspectives.

5c Individually, finish the following sentences as they would be finished by someone subscribing to the perspective in brackets after them:

'Because the decision-makers are all men . . .' (Feminist)
'By studying the doctor–patient relationship . . .' (Interactionist)
'In an egalitarian society . . .' (Functionalist)
'The point of treating a situation as "strange" is . . .' (Phenomenologist)

5d Write a similar list of five 'starts' and hand them to your fellow students to finish.

6a If you are studying in a large group, divide into five smaller groups and choose one of the following roles:

The New Right
The Marxists
The Social Democrats
The Functionalists
The Feminists

Each should come up with a set of welfare policies on the 'five giants':

inadequate education
ill health
unemployment
poor housing
poverty

6b Explain why your group thinks the old-style welfare policies (1946–79) were in need of change, and particularly why they failed to eliminate each of the five giants. Also explain how your group's new policies will work to tackle these giants.

Bibliography

Ascher, K. (1987) *The Politics of Privatisation: Contracting Out Public Services,* London: Macmillan

Baudrillard, J. (1985) 'The ecstasy of communication', in H. Foster (ed.) *Postmodern Culture,* London: Pluto

Bauman, Z. (1988) 'Is there is postmodern sociology?', *Theory, Culture and Society,* Vol. 5, pp. 217–37

Beveridge, W. (1942) *Social Insurance and Allied Services,* Cmd 6404, London: HMSO; reprinted 1984

Blaxter, M. (1987) 'Evidence on inequality in health from a national survey', *Lancet* No. 2, pp. 30–33

Boyson, R. (1975) 'Down with the poor', in E. Butterworth and R. Holman (eds) *Social Welfare in Modern Britain,* London: Fontana, pp. 381–7

Cartwright, A. and O'Brien, M. (1978) 'Social class variations in health care and in the nature of general practice consultations', in D. Tuckett and J. Kaufert (eds) *Basic Readings in Medical Sociology,* London: Tavistock

Clarke, J. *et al.* (1987) *Ideologies of Welfare,* London: Hutchinson

Cochrane, A. and Clarke, J. (eds) (1993) *Comparing Welfare States: Britain in International Context,* London: Sage

Davis, A. and Horobin, G. (eds) (1977) *Medical Encounters: The Experience of Illness and Treatment,* London: Croom Helm

Dixon, J. and Scheurell, R. (eds) (1989) *Social Welfare in Developed Market Countries,* London: Routledge

Friedmann, R. *et al.* (eds) (1987) *Modern Welfare States,* London: Harvester Wheatsheaf

Gamble, A. (1988) *Free Economy, Strong State,* London: Macmillan

Gellner, E. (1992) *Postmodernism, Reason and Religion,* London: Routledge

Gilbert, N. (1983) *Capitalism and the Welfare State,* New Haven, CT: Yale University Press

Goffman, E. (1961) *Asylums,* 1984 edn, Harmondsworth: Penguin

Gough, I. (1979) *The Political Economy of the Welfare State,* London: Macmillan

Graham, H, and Oakley, A. (1981) 'Competing ideologies of reproduction: medical and maternal perspectives on pregnancy', in H. Roberts (1981) *Women, Health and Reproduction,* London: Routledge

Gunder-Frank, A. (1980) *Crisis in the World Economy,* London: Heinemann

Jordan, B. (1987) *Rethinking Welfare,* Oxford: Blackwell

Kickert, W. (1991) 'Steering at a distance: a new paradigm in public governance in Dutch higher education' Paper for the European Consortium for Political Research, University of Essex, March

Le Grand, J. and Estrin, S. (eds) (1989) *Market Socialism,* Oxford: Oxford University Press

Mishra, R. (1981) *Society and Social Policy,* London: Macmillan

—— (1984) *The Welfare State in Crisis,* Brighton: Wheatsheaf

O'Connor, J. (1981) *The Fiscal Crisis of the State,* London: Macmillan

Open University (1985) *Health and Disease,* U205, Milton Keynes: Open University (see especially 'Studying health and disease')

Patrick, D. L. and Scrambler, G. (1986) *Sociology as Applied to Medicine,* London: Ballière Tindall

Turner, B. (1993) *Regulating Bodies,* London: Routledge

Willmott, P. and Murie, A. (1988) *Polarisation and Social Housing,* London: Policy Studies Institute

(On p. 34 document A is from Dr Rhodes Boyson; document B is from Lord Beveridge.)

3

Approaching the study of health and welfare

Figure 3.1 'Just complete this and post it back to me at the University, would you?'

What would a better method of study be here?

Table 3.1 The methods of research available to the student of health, welfare and poverty

More quantitative	More qualitative
PRIMARY DATA (collected by the researcher) this includes . . . *Asking questions*	
structured interviews closed-ended questionnaires (ie tick-the-box answers)	unstructured interviews open-ended questionnaires life histories group discussions
Observation	
non-participant observation (can be quantitative or qualitative)	participant observation
Experiments	
controlled experiments (in the laboratory – including animal studies)	uncontrolled experiments (in real situations outside the laboratory)
SECONDARY DATA (obtained from other sources)	
official statistics	diaries, letters, autobiographies, etc.

Perspectives such as those discussed in Chapter 2, and the methods outlined in Table 3.1, are linked in that some perspectives are more likely to use particular sorts of methods than others. Which of these methods are most suited to each perspective, and why?

Asking questions

Questionnaires

Closed-ended

Heartbeat Wales, a government-backed health education pilot project, has spent two years analysing a survey of Welsh families which asked people aged between 12 and 64 detailed questions on their attitudes to health, their medical history and use of health services. In total 22,000 people were covered, the largest survey of its kind in Britain.

Open-ended

For his study *Poverty in the United Kingdom* Peter Townsend used a questionnaire which combined both open- and closed-ended questions about households (see Figure 3.2, p. 40). The major survey work was conducted during 1968–9 in 51 constituencies in the UK. Follow-up surveys were conducted later in Salford, Neath, Glasgow and Belfast. In total data on 2,052 households (6,098 individuals) were successfully collected in the main survey. Examples of the open-ended questions include:

'If there is poverty, what do you think can be done about it?'

'What kinds of things have you done lately to try to get a job?'

Townsend's questionnaire was administered by researchers. What are the advantages and disadvantages of this approach compared to, say, sending it through the post?

Interviews

Structured

The Government's Health and Life-Style Survey uses in-depth interview techniques combined with measurements of blood pressure, lung function and so on. It aims to establish correlations between the nature of individuals' health and lifestyle and their income, social class, education and housing. Questions included ones on self-perceived health, ability to sleep well and so on.

Try writing closed-ended questions designed to elicit this information. Swap yours with other members of the group for constructive criticism.

Unstructured

In *Poverty: The Forgotten Englishmen* (1970) Coates and Silburn describe a study which they organised of poverty in the St Ann's district of Nottingham. The team conducted

QUESTION 14   Fuel
Everyone forgets to order coal. Stress "through lack of money".

QUESTION 15   Birthday parties
Again the emphasis is on the expense and the experience of bringing the child's friends into the home, so stress that we don't mean just a family party.

QUESTION 17(a)   Social class
This question requires the views of both chief wage-earner (head of household) and housewife. By "wage-earner" we mean the person upon whose earnings the housekeeping income primarily depends. By "head of household" we have in mind the alternative person to be questioned if there is no chief wage-earner, e.g. a husband who is a retirement pensioner, or a widowed mother (who may be the tenant) living with her widowed daughter (the housewife) and grandchildren. As far as possible the views on social class should be sought from each person independently. If both are present take the question stage by stage, making sure both answer before passing on. The question asks first for a self-rating, which must be written down. At this stage avoid putting names of classes into people's heads. People often hesitate awkwardly, so try to get the informant to say what class she thinks she belongs to or "is nearest to". Prompt by repeating the question carefully, and say "It's what you think", implying (which is true) that everyone has their own idea and each is equally valid. Do not strain to get an answer if one is not easily forthcoming. Do not assume the informant will pick one class only. Multiple choices of "middle and working" or "professional and working" are allowed.

QUESTION 17(b)   Determinant of class
Code housewife and chief wage- earner only. Next, to give us a clue as to what the informant is using as a reference point and scale we ask, in effect, the informant's idea of what determines "class".

QUESTION 17(c)   Names of classes
Third, the informant is presented with a flash-card (this is why husband and wife should if possible be interviewed separately, since otherwise the second person may be unduly influenced). Code one item only. If informant wants (again) to say "none", say 'Well, I've got to put to put something down, which would you think was nearest?" This rating is the most important bit of the question. Do not be puzzled if the wife gives a different answer from the husband. This is quite common.

QUESTION 17(d)   Father's main occupation
That is, the occupation held for most of the time (not necessarily the most recent).

QUESTION 18 Well off
Four comparisons are made in this series of questions –with relatives, with other people (note–of the same age) in locality, with the average in the country and finally in the context of time. Prompt carefully and remember that you might get a different response for one comparison than for another.

FOR ALL   CODE ALL IN HOUSEHOLD
14. Have you ever been short of fuel during the   yes
last year through lack of money? I mean   no
have you had to go without a fire on a cold   DK
day or go to bed early to keep warm or   DNA
light the fire late because of lack of coal?

ASK PARENT OF CHILD 3–14   CODE ALL CHILDREN 3–14
15. What about your son's/daughter's   DNA skip to Q.16
last birthday? Did he/she have a   yes
party with friends (not just   no
brothers and sisters)?   DK

ASK PARENT OF CHILD 3–14
16. How much altogether does he/she net in   nothing
pocket money per week, i.e only from   Write in est.
persons living in the household   amt. in shillings

ASK HOUSEWIFE & CHIEF WAGE-EARNER/HEAD OF HOUSEHOLD
17. (a) You hear of people talking about social class. If you were asked what social class you belong to, what would you say? PROMPT BY REPEATING THE QUESTION AND SAY, "It's what you say; everyone has their own view. What would be the name of the class you belong to or are nearest to?"

WRITE IN ANSWER

☐
☐

CODE HOUSEWIFE AND C.W.E. ONLY
(b) What decides what class you're in? Is it mainly:–
PROMPT AND CODE ONE ONLY

DNA skip to Q.19   2=your way of life?
Y=job?   3=money?
O=education?   4=other (SPECIFY)
1=family born into?   5=DK

(c) I have a card which has some names of classes written on it. Could you please look and say which of these you belong to? SHOW FLASHCARD No 7

X=upper middle   1=upper working   4=DK
Y=middle   2=working   5=none
O=lower middle   3=poor

(d) Some people think it goes by what your father's job was. Could you tell me your father's main job in life? And the employer's (or own) business?

WRITE IN ANSWER. IF UNSPECIFIC ASK "What did he do?"

☐
☐

ASK HOUSEWIFE & C.W.E./H.O.H.   CODE HOUSEWIFE AND C.W.E. ONLY
18. (a) How well off do you feel these days on your income? e.g, compared with the rest of your family (I mean the relatives who don't live here) would you say you are:–

PROMPT AND CODE   X=better off?   O=worse off?
ONE ONLY   Y=about the same?   1=DK

(b) Compared with other people round   2=better off?
here of your age, would you say you are:– 3=about the same?
                                          4=worse off?
                                          5=DK

(c) Compared with the average in the   X=better off?
country, would you say you are:–   Y=about the same?
                                          O=worse off?
                                          I=DK

(d) On the whole is your   2=better off than ever?
situation getting better   3=worse off than ever?
or worse? Are you:–   4=have known better/worse times?
                                  5=about the same as ever?
                                  6=DK

---

1. *Which question will enable the researchers to identify the respondents' social class according to the Registrar General's scale?*
2. *Use the following concepts to make statements about the information which would be provided by these questions: relative deprivation; absolute poverty; self-assigned class; reference group. Make your statements as specific as possible.*
3. *The instructions for question 17a are very detailed. Why do you think they have been written in such a detailed way? Why have these specific instructions been given?*

Figure 3.2 Townsend's questionnaire

Source: Townsend (1979)

interviews in three stages, the first with a sample of people of, nearly 200, the second of under 100 and the third over 200. The research was conducted between 1966 and 1968. Few details of the interview schedule are given in the book, but it is clear from quotes of the responses that it was at least partly unstructured. One old lady, on being asked to describe her financial situation, said she was 'not wealthy at all, but I just about get by. Of course, my boys are very good' (p. 60). People in the sample were also asked what 'wealth' was. They were allowed to answer as they wanted.

Life histories

Roger Sherrott (1983) interviewed 50 people who were volunteers for various sorts of charitable and other work. He took life histories from each of them, encouraging them to speak frankly about their current and past involvement in voluntary work, their social situation, their feelings and experiences. The result has been described as 'a rich portrait of volunteering'. Sherrott found that there were many motives for volunteering, from instrumental reasons (for example, to enhance employment prospects) to normative ones (the belief in the need for a strong community) to moral ones (volunteering as a means of doing one's duty to God or society).

What are the strengths and weaknesses of the 'life histories' approach?

Group discussions

Barbara Mostyn (1983) also conducted a study of volunteering, first using group discussions, and later with semi-structured interviews. For the first phase, houses were selected at random in a particular area, the people inside were told about the study, they were given a questionnaire about their involvement in voluntary work and, if they qualified to join in terms of their class and age (because a mixed group of participants was required), asked if they would be willing to take part in a group discussion on volunteering. In the second phase these discussions were held in community halls hired for the occasion. There were a total of six separate discussion groups, three in York and three in London. There were a total of 46 people attending. Mostyn found that most respondents agreed on the following hierarchy of status in voluntary agencies and volunteering:

Altruistic volunteering, e.g. Samaritans, mountain rescue, St John's Ambulance

Helping people in distress, e.g. Salvation Army, fostering

Giving aid to the less fortunate, e.g. Citizens Advice Bureau, Friends of the Hospital, Round Table

Improving society, e.g. youth leaders, school governors, residents' associations

Self-interest, e.g. trade union work, party activists, local pressure groups

Observation

Participant observation

The authors of the book *A Cycle of Deprivation?* (Coffield *et al.* 1980) decided that participant observation of 'deprived' families was the best way to understand the nature and causes of their deprivation. Accordingly they studied four carefully chosen families in 'Kindleton' (somewhere in the English Midlands) over a period of two years in the mid-1970s:

> 'We were temporary participant-observers entering the lives of our families, sometimes for a short visit and on other occasions for a whole day; at times we just talked to members of the families and at other times joined a birthday party, a family christening or other family celebrations.'

Their finding was that the concept of a 'cycle of deprivation' (see p. 63 for an explanation of this) is too simple to explain the lives of the four families they studied. A 'web' of deprivation is a more adequate metaphor. The authors stressed the complexity of the families' situations and the fact that the multiple deprivations they suffered were interacting and cumulative:

> 'We would claim that no single hypothesis and no group of simple hypotheses could hope to explain the intricate mesh of factors which we have listed when summarizing the crucial features of any one family at the end of each chapter.'

1 *What are:*
   – the advantages
   – the disadvantages
   of the choice of participant observation as the research method for this study?
2 *Given that a non-sociologist such as George Orwell could use this method (for his book* Down and Out in Paris and London*) and that the results of the method read more like newspaper journalism than a scientific account, is there any point in studying sociology if participant observation is the method you decide to use?*
3 *Participant observation can be overt or covert. Under what circumstances would covert participant observation be advisable, and why?*

Non-participant observation

The earliest studies of poverty tended to use non-participant observation (NPO) in assessing its nature and extent. Charles Booth's *Life and Labour of the People in London* (1891–1902; see Fried and Elman 1969) is an example of the indirect use of non-participant observation. Booth met the London School Board visitors responsible for the East End, the area he was interested in. These officials visited homes in the area and kept very detailed written accounts of every family with children of school age or pre-school age there. Thus Booth was able to gain a clear picture of conditions at the end of the nineteenth century using NPO by a team of trained and skilled workers.

What are the advantages and disadvantages of Booth's approach?

Experiments

Controlled experiments

These attempt to keep all important conditions constant and usually have two identical groups for testing: the *experimental* and, for comparison, the *control*. One variable is introduced or changed in the experimental group but not the control. Any subsequent differences between the two should therefore be the result of that change. In tests of the effectiveness of a medicine, it is administered to the experimental group; the control group, who are usually matched in terms of age, health, etc., are given a *placebo* – some 'treatment' which is known to be ineffective. The point in doing this is that receiving treatment of any kind can sometimes have an effect on the patient. Administering a placebo means that both are receiving some treatment. It is best if the experiment is a 'double blind' one, that is, neither the experimenters nor the subjects of the experiment know who is receiving the medicine and who the placebo.

Controlled experiments have been conducted to test the effectiveness of alternative medicine. One was a test of acupuncture's ability to control disabling breathlessness. Twelve matched pairs of patients with this problem were selected. One of each of the pairs was given acupuncture treatment, the other placebo acupuncture (i.e. what appeared to be acupuncture but was not). After three weeks' treatment those people who had received acupuncture felt significantly greater benefit than those who were given the placebo.

Experiments on young animals have tested the effect of malnutrition on brain growth. Control and experimental animals were kept in laboratory conditions, the latter being deprived of adequate food for long periods of time. Later analysis of the brains of both sets of animals showed that the experimental group had fewer and smaller brain cells than normal. It seems that malnutrition during the period of most rapid brain growth (the first six months after birth) can irrevocably result in this deficiency.

> *What factors make controlled experiments in sociology more difficult and unreliable than those in the natural sciences?*

Uncontrolled experiments

This sort of experiment is uncontrolled in the sense that not all conditions are kept constant. The experimental and control groups are not identical, nor are the conditions in which they exist. One study in the Birmingham area looked at a sample of boys between 6 and 7 and another between 10 and 11. Some of the boys were from severely deprived large families known to the social services department. The rest (the control group) lived in the same area but were not under social services supervision. Differences such as height, visual impairment, hearing loss, disease and so on were examined. It was found that the experimental group (the ones known to social services) tended to be shorter, were more often ill and were more likely to suffer poor vision and hearing than the control group.

Primary and secondary data

Primary data means data which has been collected by the researcher specifically for the purposes of the research and which did not exist before. Secondary data is also used by the researcher, but it was already in existence, having been collected for other or more general purposes. *Qualitative* secondary datas consist of personal accounts, comments, stories, etc.

Secondary data

The three methods of collecting evidence specifically for the purposes of a particular sociological inquiry that we have examined above are said to provide *primary* data. In addition, sociologists may draw upon *secondary* data.

Statistics

We can infer levels of health and illness from official statistics. There are four categories of these:

1 mortality statistics, such as the infant mortality rate (IMR);

2 statistics on the use of health facilities (e.g. the Hospital In-Patient Enquiry – HIPE) or studies of GPs' case loads;

3 statistics on sickness absence from work;

4 statistics collected from official surveys. These include the General Household Survey, an annual survey of a representative sample of people in Britain, and the National Food Survey, a questionnaire sent annually to a sample of the population by the Ministry of Agriculture.

The longitudinal study published by the Office of Population Censuses and Surveys (OPCS) uses a combination of statistical sources. It has followed vital events in the lives of a sample of 1 per cent of the population of England and Wales since 1971. These include births, marriages, deaths, cancer registrations and so on, all of which can be gleaned from official sources of information such as the Census, registrations by doctors, registrars and others, all of which are collated by the OPCS.

Each of the four categories of statistics has its problems:

Mortality statistics measure only deaths (mortality), not illness (morbidity), and so non-fatal diseases are hidden from view.

Statistics on the use of health facilities only catch the people who have gone through the process of recognition, definition and action (see p. 2).

Statistics on sickness absence from work exclude those not working (for whatever reason), and disregard those who are absent for less than seven days as short absences do not qualify for sickness benefit and are therefore not recorded.

Information collected from the General Household Survey tends to underestimate such problems as cancer and mental illness because people are asked about their own health.

Problems such as a high non-response rate (which particularly affects the National Food Survey), limited sample sizes and difficulties in selecting a truly representative sample mean that there are usually question marks over the statistical significance of results.

The time taken to collate the results often means that statistics are out of date by the time they become available.

Political expediency can influence official statistics in many ways. The changing definition of 'the unemployed' is the best-known example of how official statistics can be manipulated. For example, after 1982 only those who claimed unemployment benefit were counted as unemployed (as opposed to those registered for work). This change 'reduced' unemployment by 170,000 at a stroke.

The government can delay the publication of any statistical work it might find embarrassing. It can also limit the number of copies available to the public or try to hush the matter up altogether. This occurred to a study of primary school staff begun in 1987 by the Department of Education and Science and to two surveys on inequalities in health.

More generally, the statistics encapsulate medical definitions and diagnoses of ill-health. Each case is different, but doctors have to label them as they have been trained to do. A death, particularly in old age, may be the result of many interlinked factors yet the doctor must state a cause, which then becomes a statistic. Moreover, it is unlikely that a doctor would register a cause of death such as 'stressful and dangerous work conditions', although in a sense these could be said to cause death.

Despite these problems researchers have been able to use official statistics in their research. Brian Abel-Smith and Peter Townsend (1965) used figures collected for other purposes by government departments to show that the numbers of those in poverty (defined as 40 per cent above the level of National Assistance Benefit) had increased from 4 million in 1953/4 to 7.5 million in 1960, casting doubt on the government's assertion to the British people that 'you've never had it so good'.

> *What are the advantages for the researcher of using statistics?*

Statistics are useful because the researcher may be able to use the comparative method, that is, the comparison of different countries' statistics to identify the importance of factors that differ between them. Durkheim's use of suicide statistics is a well-known example in sociology. He claimed to show that societies and communities which have a high level of social integration also have a low level of suicide. So, using statistics, he claimed that too low a level of integration caused a high suicide rate.

Figure 3.3 Correlation between colon cancer incidence and meat consumption (1975)

> *Study Figures 3.3 and 3.4, which are both based on official statistics. What do these graphs seem to show? Why might this conclusion be incorrect? (Think about the difference between correlation and causation.)*

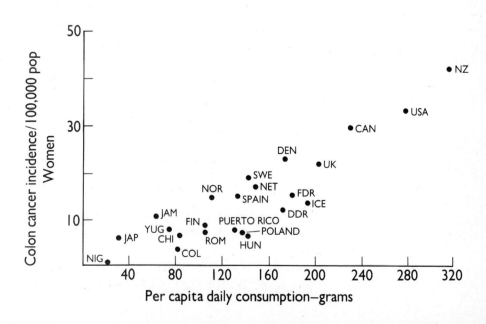

Figure 3.4
Correlation
between breast
cancer mortality
and fat
consumption

Source: Doll
and Peto
(1981)

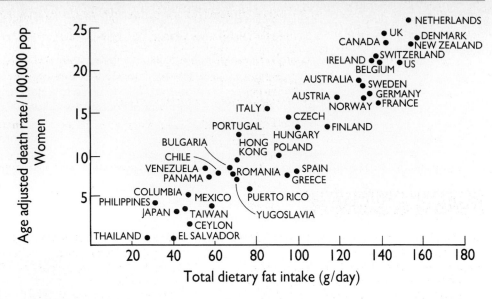

Qualitative secondary data

For *Adolescent Boys of East London* (1966) Peter Willmott asked some of the boys he was studying to keep a week's diary. Thirty of them wrote a diary during the same week in 1966 and were given £2 for doing so. Willmott gave them some instructions about the sort of thing he wanted them to write, and an example for them to follow. Later he was able to use this data to describe the lives of the boys. His aim was to examine the processes of male adolescence, especially among the working class. 'Girls', he states, 'pose less of a problem to adult society', as presumably do the middle class.

1 *Comment on Wilmott's statement and on the titles:* Adolescent Boys of East London *and* Poverty: The Forgotten Englishmen.
   What are the advantages and disadvantages of Willmott's 'diary method'?

Joan Higgins (1988) wrote:

> 'I began this book because of a deep commitment to the fundamental principle upon which the NHS was based, that access to health care should not be based upon the ability to pay the costs of treatment, especially during periods of sickness. This was accompanied by a growing anxiety that changes in the private sector since 1979 had undermined that principle. Most of what I have seen and heard in the research for the book has confirmed that view . . .'

2a *In what ways, specifically, might the prior values held by a researcher influence the course of their research? (Think about the different stages of research: choice of subject, development of a hypothesis, choice of method, analysis of results and so on). Give examples to illustrate your points.*

2b *How could the research be made as objective as possible, so that the results would be the same irrespective of the prior views of the researcher?*

3   Which methods would be most suitable for studying the following subjects:

- *lifestyle and poverty in the gypsy community;*

- *the relationship between deaths of pensioners during the winter from hypothermia and the levels of state benefits they receive;*

- *the effectiveness of social workers;*

- *the influence of drug companies' advertising and promotion campaigns on doctors' prescribing habits.*

Bibliography

Abel-Smith, B. and Townsend, P. (1965) *The Poor and the Poorest,* London: Bell

Brennan, M. E. (1973) 'Medical characteristics of children supervised by the local authority social services department', *Policy and Politics,* Vol. 1, No. 3, p. 255

Coates, K. and Silburn, R. (1970) *Poverty: The Forgotten Englishmen,* Harmondsworth: Penguin

Coffield, F. *et al.* (1980) *A Cycle of Deprivation?* London: Heinemann

DHSS/DSS (annual) *Health and Personal Social Services Statistics for England,* London: HMSO

Davis, A .and Horobin, G. (eds) (1977)*Medical Encounters: The Experience of Illness and Treatment,* London: Croom Helm

Doll, R. and Peto, R. (1981) *The Causes of Cancer,* Oxford: Oxford University Press

Fried, A. and Elman, M. (1969) *Charles Booth's London,* London: Hutchinson

Fry, J., Brooks, D. and McColl, I. (1984) *The NHS Data Book,* Lancaster: MTP Press

Gardner, M. J. *et al.* (n.d.) *Atlas of Mortality from Selected Diseases in England and Wales 1968–1978,* Chichester: John Wiley & Sons

—— (n.d.) *Atlas of Cancer Mortality in England and Wales 1968–1978,* Chichester: John Wiley & Sons

Grant, N. and Middleton, N. (1984) *The Daily Telegraph Atlas of the World Today,* London: Daily Telegraph

Hartley, L. (1988) *The History of Medicine,* Oxford: Blackwell

Hatch, S. (1983) *Volunteers: Patterns, Meanings and Motives,* Berkhamstead: Volunteer Centre

Kane, E. (1984) *Doing Your Own Research,* London: Marion Boyars

Kidron, M. and Segal, R. (1984) *The State of the World Atlas,* London: Pluto

Kurian, G. T. (1979) *The Book of World Ratings,* London: Macmillan

Mostyn, B. (1983) 'The meaning of voluntary work', in Hatch (1983)

Office of Health Economics (1984) *Compendium of Health Statistics,* 5th edn, London: OHE

Open University (1985) *Health and Disease,* U205 (see especially 'Studying health and disease')

Radical Statistics Health Group (1987) *Facing the Figures,* London: Radical Statistics

Robinson, T. (1978) *Worlds Apart: Professionals and Their Clients in the Welfare State,* London:Bedford Square Press

Sherrott, R. (1983) 'Fifty volunteers', in Hatch (1983)

Townsend, P. (1979) *Poverty in the United Kingdom,* Harmondsworth: Penguin

United Nations (annual) *Statistical Yearbook* and *Demographic Yearbook,* New York: United Nations

Willmott, P. (1966) *Adolescent Boys of East London,* London: Routledge & Kegan Paul

World Health Organisation (annual) *World Health Statistics,* London: HMSO

4 ▸ Poverty

Figure 4.1 A mother and child living in basic conditions

Either alone or in groups, describe the circumstances in which someone could be said to be living 'in poverty'. Compare your descriptions with others in the group.

What is poverty?

There are three main ways of defining of poverty:

1 Absolute poverty

2 Relative poverty

3 Poverty of lifestyle

Absolute poverty

According to this definition, poverty means having inadequate income for food, clothing and shelter. Early researchers into poverty used this definition; the most important of these writers were Seebohm Rowntree, whose study of York,

Poverty: A Study of Town Life, was published in 1901, and Charles Booth, whose *Life and Labour of the People of London* was published in 17 volumes in 1902.

Rowntree's definition of poverty was based on the idea of a measurable subsistence poverty line, below which one did not have the necessities of life. He calculated

> 'what income is required by families of different sizes to provide the minimum of food, clothing (second hand) and shelter needed for the maintenance of merely physical health'.

If a family fell below this line, then they were poor. In those days 17p was enough to feed one man for a day (10p for a child), though this required one to buy from the cheapest shop. To be classified as being in 'primary poverty' a family

> 'must never purchase a half penny newspaper or spend a penny to buy a ticket for a popular concert. They must write no letters . . . they must never contribute anything to their church or chapel . . . the children must have no pocket money . . . the father must smoke no tobacco and must drink no beer.'

'Secondary poverty' was the condition in which a family did have enough money to live but they wasted some of it. Rowntree did not necessarily blame the poor for wasting their money. He said their circumstances were often so bad that it was not surprising they turned to drink or some other expensive habit.

Booth also adopted a harsh definition of poverty, though there are elements of an understanding of relative poverty in his definition (these are italicised):

> 'By the word "poor" I mean . . . those who have a sufficiently regular though bare income . . . and by "very poor" those who from any cause fall much below this standard. The "poor" are those whose means may be sufficient but are barely sufficient for *decent independent life,* the "very poor" those whose means are insufficient for this *according to the usual standard of life in this country.* My "poor" may be described as living under a struggle to obtain the necessaries of life and make both ends meet, while the "very poor" live in a state of chronic want.'

Relative poverty

According to Kenneth Galbraith (1962):

> 'People are poverty stricken when their income, even if it is adequate for survival, falls markedly below that of the community. Then they cannot have what the larger community regards as the minimum necessary for decency; and they cannot wholly escape, therefore, the judgement of the larger community that they are indecent. They are degraded for, in the literal sense, they live outside the grades or categories which the community regards as acceptable.'

List the things that in Britain today comprise the 'minimum necessary for decency'. If you are working in a group, compare your lists.

Relative poverty, then, is the state of being poor relative to the community in which one lives. This may result in rejection by the community. It need not necessarily lead

Figure 4.2 A poor family in the early 1900s

to a *feeling* of being poor, though. The subjective experience of deprivation, termed 'relative deprivation' by W. G. Runciman (1969) depends on who one compares oneself to – one's 'reference group':

> 'relative deprivation should always be understood to mean a sense of deprivation; a person who is "relatively deprived" need not be "objectively" deprived in the more usual sense'.

It is harder to put a precise figure on relative poverty than it is for absolute poverty. Two attempts have been as follows:

Brian Abel-Smith and Peter Townsend (1965) used the government's minimum level of benefit and added another 40 per cent. In those days this benefit was called National Assistance Benefit (NAB); it became Supplementary Benefit and then Income Support. In 1994 a couple receiving Income Support were eligible to receive £71.70 plus various other benefits (Housing Benefit, free school meals, prescriptions, etc.). Abel-Smith and Townsend would consider this to be the absolute poverty line. Adding 40 per cent would define a relative poverty line for British society today – for such a couple an income of £100.38.

In his more recent *Poverty in the United Kingdom* (1979) Townsend suggested another way of arriving at a figure for relative poverty: taking the average income and dividing it by two. Thus having an income which is less than half the average person's income would classify a person as living in relative poverty.

In 1985 the average gross weekly income for various categories of workers was as follows:

Men (manual)	£163.60
Men (non-manual)	£225
Women (manual)	£101.30
Women (non-manual)	£133.80
All	£177.00

What problems are there with the notion that you are living in relative poverty if the 'larger community' considers you to be living in an unacceptable way?

Poverty of lifestyle

This approach to measuring poverty takes into account not just financial factors but also a person's lifestyle. The idea is that two people may be on the same income (a low one), but only one may have a circle of friends, many interests, plenty of facilities nearby and so on. The other is isolated, perhaps in a depressing inner-city environment, with no social contacts and no facilities available. One is in poverty, but the other is not.

Townsend (1979) tried to take such factors into account by giving his sample of respondents a structured interview about their leisure activities and other factors. By using an appropriate scoring system he was able to assign an 'index of poverty' to them. Some of the things he asked them about are listed in Table 4.1.

Table 4.1 Townsend's deprivation index

Characteristic	Percentage of the population
1. Has not had a week's holiday away from home in the last 12 months	53.6
2. (Adults only) Has not had a relative or friend to the home for a meal or snack in the last four weeks	33.4
3. (Adults only) Has not been out in the last four weeks to a relative or friend for a meal or snack	45.1
4. (Children under 15 only) Has not had a friend to play or to tea in the last four weeks	36.3
5. (Children only) Did not have a party on last birthday	55.6
6. Has not had an afternoon or evening out for entertainment in the last two weeks	47.0
7. Does not have fresh meat (including meals out) as many as four days a week	19.3
8. Has gone through one or more days in the past fortnight without a cooked meal	7.0
9. Has not had a cooked breakfast most days of the week	67.3
10. Household does not have a refrigerator	45.1
11. Household does not usually have a Sunday joint (three in four times)	25.9
12. Household does not have sole use of four amenities indoors (flush WC; sink or washbasin and cold water tap; fixed bath or shower; and gas or electric cooker)	21.4

Townsend found that people on lower incomes tended to have a proportionately high 'index of poverty'. He discovered a threshold of income, below which there was a sudden increase in poverty of lifestyle as measured by the index. This was 1.5 times the Supplementary Benefit level.

What problems can you see with this approach to poverty?

One of the main difficulties with this deprivation index is that people may score highly on it not because they are deprived but because they choose not to (for example) have a cooked breakfast most days of the week. In a more recent study Mack and Lansley (1985) attempted to distinguish between styles of living that people could not afford and those they did not choose. One way they did this was by using a similar questionnaire to Townsend's but asking their respondents whether they went without a particular item by choice or because they could not afford it.

Mack and Lansley also tried to establish how far there was agreement between people on what the necessities of life are. They found that there was a large measure of agreement on this. They used this agreed list of necessities (see Table 4.2) to define poverty: lack of three or more items rendered one 'poor'. (They excluded things like a television, which very few people lack, and a garden and access to public transport, which will be affected by which part of the country one lives in.) They concluded that 7.5 million people (13.8 per cent of the population) lived in poverty in 1983 – a lower figure than Townsend's 12.46 million (22.9 per cent) in 1968–9.

1a In small teams, prepare the following for presentation to your class:

The Economic and Social Research Council (ESRC) wants a study of poverty conducted in your area. It is offering a grant of £20,000 to do it. The report must be presented in three months' time. You are a team of sociologists and wish to be considered for the project. You therefore have to present a research proposal to the ESRC for their consideration. Your tasks are as follows:

- *Decide how you will select your sample of people to study.*

- *Decide on an appropriate definition or definitions of poverty so that you can establish how much of it exists in the area. Give a detailed rationale for your choice and explain why you rejected other alternatives.*

- *Decide which research method or methods you will use to conduct the research (see Chapter 3). Again, a detailed rationale must be given to the ESRC.*

- *Give your research team a name (linked to a university or college?), elect a spokesperson and prepare any visual aids (overhead projector transparencies, photocopied handouts) you need to present your proposal.*

1b While each group makes its presentation the others in the class become the members of the ESRC (respected professors and such). They should try to establish, through questions, which research group to select.

2 How far does your perception of 'necessities' agree with the general public's? Rank the list in Table 4.2 in order of importance. Then compare your results with Mack and Lansley's findings (for which, consult Table 4.7 on page 69).

Examination question

'Despite many sociological studies on poverty, it is still not possible to define a "poverty line" which will be supported by all.' Critically examine the arguments for and against this view.

AEB A-level Paper 2, Summer 1994, question 6

Table 4.2 Mack and Lansley's jumbled list of necessities

New, not second-hand clothes	A holiday away from home for one week a year, not with relatives	A roast meat joint or its equivalent once a week
Heating to warm living areas of the of the home if it's cold	Public transport for one's needs	A 'best' outfit for special occasions
Enough bedrooms for every child over 10 of different sex to have his/her own	A garden	An outing for children once a week
Leisure equipment for children e.g. sports equipment or a bicycle	A television	Meat or fish every other day
Carpets in living rooms and bedrooms	A night out once a fortnight (adults)	A dressing gown
Presents for friends or family once a year	Celebrations on special occasions such as Christmas	Indoor toilet (not shared with another household)
Three meals a day for children	Damp-free home	Friends/family round for a meal once a month
Toys for children	A warm water-proof coat	Beds for everyone in the household
Refrigerator	Two hot meals a day (for adults)	Self-contained accommodation
Bath (not shared with another household)	A telephone	A washing machine
A car	A packet of cigarettes every other day	Two pairs of all-weather shoes

Poverty in the UK: some evidence

In July 1988 the Select Committee on Social Services published a report on the extent of poverty in Britain. This was based on official figures and used the lowest level of means-tested benefits as the marker of poverty. The report stated that:

- in 1979 4.4 million people were claiming means-tested benefits;
- by 1988 there were 8.2 million;
- in 1988 1 million were below this supposed minimum level.

However, ministers replied that these figures did not demonstrate any increase in poverty in Britain, merely the fact that eligibility for means-tested benefit had relaxed and that levels of benefits had increased. The real measure of poverty should be the poor's spending power, according to the government. This has increased. It is clear, though, that in Britain there is a growing gap between the poor and the better off (see Figure 4.3 on p. 55).

The Joseph Rowntree Foundation Inquiry into Income and Wealth (Barclay *et al.* 1995), conducted in the early 1990s, found:

The poorest 20–30 per cent of the population have failed to share in economic growth since 1979.

The experience of poverty and exclusion is much higher among the non-white population.

Income inequality grew faster in the UK during the 1980s than in almost any other comparable country.

There is a growing polarisation between 'work rich' and 'work poor' households. The proportion of two adult-earner households rose between 1975 and 1993 by 9 per cent to 60 per cent; the proportion of households with no adult earner also rose from 3 per cent to 11 per cent in the same period.

18 per cent of the white population were in the poorest 20 per cent, compared to 34 per cent of the non-white population. Over 40 per cent of West Indians and 50 per cent of Pakistanis/Bangladeshis are in this group. Indians, by contrast, are disproportionately found in the middle and second highest 20 per cent groups.

Table 4.3 is of particular interest because it combines three aspects of stratification: class, ethnicity and gender. What patterns does is show, and how might these be linked to poverty?

Table 4.3 People in employment, by ethnic group, socioeconomic group and gender, Spring 1994

	Black	Indian	Ethnic group Pakistani or Bangladeshi	Other ethnic minority groups	All ethnic minority groups	White	All persons
Males							
Professional	–	13.7	–	19.5	11.7	8.2	8.4
Intermediate	25.2	30.5	18.3	28.2	26.3	31.1	30.9
Skilled non-manual	13.7	13.5	15.7	16.8	14.7	11.6	11.8
Skilled manual	28.9	22.3	33.5	19.2	25.3	31.6	31.3
Partly skilled	17.2	17.0	22.9	11.1	16.9	13.4	13.5
Unskilled	9.4	–	–	–	5.1	4.1	4.1
All males (=100%) (thousands)	144	190	110	126	571	12,887	13,458
Females							
Professional	–	7.0	–	–	4.8	2.6	2.6
Intermediate	35.1	23.2	28.7	30.9	29.4	30.3	30.3
Skilled non-manual	28.8	34.2	40.7	35.9	33.5	37.0	36.8
Skilled manual	9.6	–	–	–	8.1	8.1	8.1
Partly skilled	14.2	26.7	–	13.0	18.7	15.5	15.7
Unskilled	9.7	–	–	–	5.5	6.6	6.5
All females (thousands)(=100%)*	147	152	45	103	443	10,272	10,715

* Includes members of the armed forces and those who did not give ethnic group or occupation.

Source: Social Trends 25, London: HMSO (1995), Table 1.9, p. 20

Figure 4.3 Changes in real income, 1979–92 (% changes in income after housing costs)

Source: Households Below Average Income, London: HMSO (1994); reproduced in *Sociology Update 1995,* p. 15

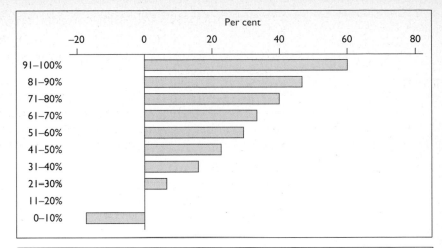

Figure 4.4 The poor left behind

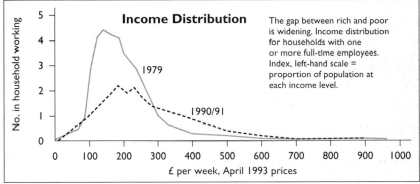

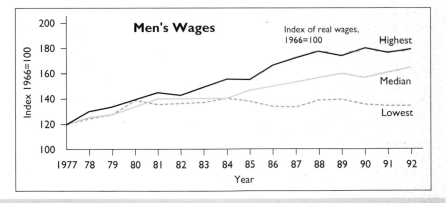

What trends does Table 4.4 demonstrate?

Table 4.4 Unemployment rates by ethnic origin, Great Britain, 1985 and 1988 (percentages)

	1985	1988
All people of working age	10.7	8.7
White	10.3	8.5
West Indian/Guyanese	21	14.9
Indian	17	11.9
Pakistani/Bangladeshi	31	24
All other ethnic origins	17	9.7

Source: Social Trends 19

Figure 4.5 International
inequality

Source: Guardian, 10
February 1995, p. 7

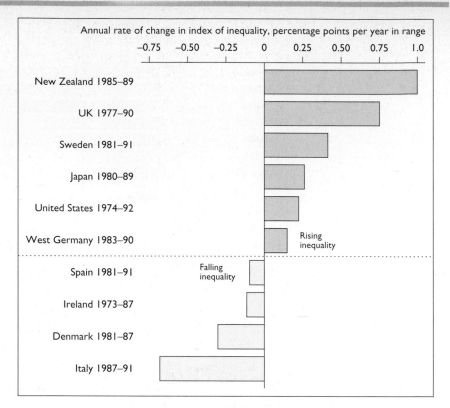

Some of the causes of the growing inequality which the Joseph Rowntree Foundation
identifies are:

- the rise in unemployment during the 1980s;

- the decline in the value of income support;

- the rise in the number of single parents;

- differential wage growth across the income spectrum, with limited growth at the
  bottom. (Wages for the lowest paid were lower in real terms in 1992 than in
  1975.)

However, the Institute for Fiscal Studies rejects the idea that the poor became
poorer during the 1980s. Gosling and others (1994) conducted a study based on
information from more than 200,000 households in Britain. They agree that those in
the lowest income bracket had less money in 1992 than in 1975: average real income
dropped by 18 per cent between 1979 and 1992 for the poorest 10 per cent of the
population, for example, and the real rate of pay for the lowest 10 per cent of men
did not change; however, their research suggests that different people are involved in
these two years. Around half of the poorest 10 per cent escape from poverty each
year. These people, many of them pensioners, enjoyed a rise in their income, from
£92 to £134 per week, while those who remained in the poorest 10 per cent saw an
average rise of only £3 per week. The worst off had an average income of £84 per
week.

The School for Advanced Urban Studies (1993) conducted a study of wealth and deprivation across the UK using the findings of the 1991 Census. They took six indicators of deprivation from the Census data: unemployment, youth unemployment, lone parenthood, single pensioners, long-term limiting illness and dependants per household. A second index used four indicators: more than one person per room, households with no car, households lacking basic amenities and households with no central heating.

What criticisms can be made of these measures of deprivation?

Their findings illustrate that the North–South divide is as present as ever:

Of the 20 most socially deprived districts, seven are inner-London districts (Hackney being the most deprived of these, and the fourth most deprived nationally) and 12 are in the North (Knowsley was the most deprived of these, and the most deprived nationally, followed by Liverpool and Manchester).

The least deprived areas were predominantly in the South East. The most northerly district in the 'top 20' was Blaby in Leicestershire.

Only 2.9 per cent of the households in Stevenage, Hertfordshire, and Basildon, Essex, were without central heating compared to 48.2 per cent in Liverpool and a national average of 17 per cent.

Table 4.5 The best-off and the worst-off districts

Most deprived districts
(Max score 6)

Knowsley	5.08
Manchester	4.99
Liverpool	4.97
Hackney	4.79
Tower Hamlets	4.46

Least deprived districts

Wokingham	1.60
Hart	1.77
Surrey Heath	1.79
Newbury	1.95
Scily Isles	1.95

Most households with no car (%)

Hackney	61.7
Tower Hamlets	61.6
Islington	59.9
Southwark	58.0
Westminster	57.7

Highest home ownership (%)

Castle Point	89.4
Rochford	86.4
Fareham	86.0
Oadby & Wigston	65.8
Blaby	85.7

table continued over

Lowest home ownership (%)

Tower Hamlets	23.2
Islington	26.7
Hackney	26.9
Southwark	27.2
Camden	33.8

Lowest home ownership (%)

Tower Hamlets	23.2
Islington	26.7
Hackney	26.9
Southwark	27.2
Camden	33.8

Most lone parent households (%)

Knowsley	9.0
Manchester	8.6
Hackney	8.4
Southwark	8.2
Lambeth	8.2

Most long term illness

(100 = average, standardised for age)

Easington	191.24
Barnsley	157.17
Knowsley	155.42
Sunderland	154.61
Manchester	152.98

Most pensioners (% population)

Eastbourne	24.0
Rother	23.5
Worthing	23.4
Arun	21.9
Christchurch	21.9

Population growth 1981-91 (%)

Milton Keynes	39.2
Wokingham	20.1
Redditch	15.8
Selby	15.1
South Hams	15.0

Source: Guardian, 10 August 1993, p. 2

Figure 4.6 Real household disposable income, United Kingdom (percentages)

Source: Social Trends 25, Figure 5.1, p. 83

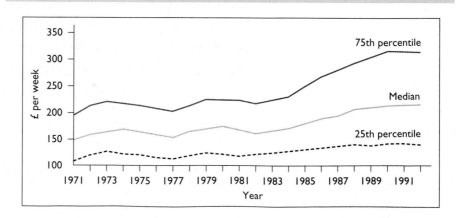

Table 4.6 Distribution of wealth, United Kingdom (percentages)

	1976	1981	1986	1991	1992
Marketable wealth					
Percentage of wealth owned by*					
Most wealthy 1%	21	18	18	17	18
Most wealthy 5%	38	36	36	34	37
Most wealthy 10%	50	50	50	46	49
Most wealthy 25%	71	73	73	70	72
Most wealthy 50%	92	92	90	92	92
Total marketable wealth					
(£ billion)	280	565	955	1,801	1,811
Marketable wealth less value of dwellings					
Percentage of wealth owned by*					
Most wealthy 1%	29	26	25	29	29
Most wealthy 5%	47	45	46	51	53
Most wealthy 10%	57	56	58	64	65
Most wealthy 25%	73	74	75	80	82
Most wealthy 50%	88	87	89	93	94

*Applies to adult population aged 18 and over.

Source: *Social Trends 25*, Table 5.23, p. 96

It is now recognised that the statistical value of the 1991 Census is limited by the fact that a significant number of people, especially in the poorest groups, failed to return their Census forms for fear of being taken to court for non-payment of the Poll Tax.

1 What implications might this have for data about income and wealth?

2 What does Figure 4.6 tell us? What other information about real household disposable income would be useful if we wish to track changes in poverty over time?

3 Using the data provided in Table 4.6, decide whether each of the following statements is true, false or impossible to say:

a The most wealthy 50 per cent increased their share of the wealth between 1976 and 1992 if marketable dwellings are included.

b The percentage of wealth owned by the least wealthy 50 per cent remained stable between 1976 and 1992 if marketable dwellings are included.

c The rich got richer between 1976 and 1992.

d The poor got poorer between 1976 and 1992.

e The very rich did better between 1976 and 1992 than the moderately rich.

(The answers are given at the end of the chapter.)

To summarise the available evidence on poverty in the UK, the groups most likely to be poor are as follows:

- the elderly
- single-parent families
- the unemployed
- the sick and the disabled
- low wage earners
- those with large families and low incomes.

Explaining poverty

Definitions and explanations of poverty are closely linked to the perspectives we examined earlier. Those which have particularly addressed the issue of poverty are: the New Right, the Social Democrats, Marxists, (and exponents of other conflict perspectives) and functionalists.

 Take each of these four perspectives and show how they might explain the persistence of poverty. If you are working in a large group, divide into smaller groups and take one perspective each. Prepare to explain its view on poverty to the others in the group.

The New Right

The New Right adopts an absolute definition of poverty and sees it as the fault of the poor people themselves. The poor have a 'culture of poverty'. Oscar Lewis (1964) argued that people who have a culture of poverty:

have a low level of literacy and education;

do not belong to trade unions;

do not join political parties;

make little use of banks, hospitals, etc.;

are critical of education and the police;

are poorly organised;

feel marginalised, helpless and dependent;

desire immediate gratification rather than deferring it;

cannot plan for the future;

are fatalistic (do not believe they can improve the situation);

believe in male superiority;

are provincial and have no sense of history.

 Do you agree that poor people in Britain have these characteristics? Are there any other features that could be said to comprise a 'culture of poverty' in the UK?

This attitude to the poor is evident in Margaret Thatcher's talk of the 'dependency culture' which she saw as one of the ills of the Welfare State resulting from the over-

Figure 4.7 Rab C Nesbitt: 'I am social scum!'

protectiveness of the 'nanny state'. She wanted to replace it with what she called the 'enterprise culture'. Similarly former junior health minister Edwina Currie blamed the relatively poorer health of those in the North on certain cultural traits, particularly diet and the habit of smoking (and on their ignorance).

The underclass

This term describes a sub-category of the poor. This group comes from a lower social class backgrounds, has a high rate of unemployment, receives welfare support from the State and is prone to high rates of crime and delinquency. The idea of an 'underclass' is also linked with the idea of a 'dependency culture' or 'culture of poverty'. The term has been criticised for its implication that the victim is to blame. Wider issues like government policy on employment need to be taken into account when discussing the very poor.

Researchers like Charles Murray (1984) who subscribe to a New Right approach believe that an 'underclass' is emerging in Britain. The idea has also caught on in the popular imagination as a result of media reporting of riots and crime in some areas of large cities. Relative geographical and social isolation has become a feature of some urban estates built in the late 1950s and 1960s. Essentially Murray's thesis involves the following points:

Members of the underclass are largely poor because of their own attitudes and behaviour: for example, they are unwilling to take on employment and tend to have children outside of stable relationships.

They are often involved in crime. They are socialised to regard this as both normal and acceptable.

Government policy has helped perpetuate the underclass. For example, the 1977 Homeless Persons Act gave pregnant women and mothers priority on council housing lists. According to Murray (and politicians subscribing to the New Right perspective) this encouraged women deliberately to have children as an escape from their parents, causing family break-up and ensnaring the women in a poverty trap.

Murray's thesis is not altogether new. It shares many elements with the 'culture of poverty' theory that was popular in the 1950s and early 1960s. His view of crime also brings to mind Walter Miller's (1962) theory of criminal working-class subcultures.

Critics of this approach have argued that it blames the victim for the circumstances they are forced to live in. It has also been noted that parents living in poverty do not bring up their children in the manner described by 'culture of poverty' theorists. Such parents are usually very keen that their children should have a better life than they had.

A report by the National Youth Agency (Wilkinson 1995) confirms this point of view. Based on interviews with 250 youngsters, it found a large number of alienated youths in Sunderland, Tyne and Wear. These young people tended to drop out of school after the age of 12 or 13, were involved in crime and had backgrounds of poverty and homelessness. Extrapolating from the data, the author of the report, Dr Clive Wilkinson, suggests that there could be as many as 100,000 members of this 'youth underclass' in Britain. However, he points to parental unemployment and deprived conditions at home as the underlying causes rather than deviant subcultures, as Murray does.

According to the New Right model:

Who or what is to blame for the existence of poverty?
What needs to be done to abolish it?
Has anything like this been done so far?

Social Democrats

The Social Democratic approach adopts a relative definition of poverty and accepts the poverty-trap (or cycle of deprivation) explanation. This suggests that people can get into a situation of poverty and, once there, find it very difficult to get out.

Paradoxically it is expensive to be poor, and those in poverty have to spend a lot just to maintain their current standard of living. For example:

The poor cannot afford to insulate their homes and so have to pay high fuel bills.

They cannot afford to travel to cheap supermarkets out of town and so have to buy goods at the expensive local corner shop.

They have to buy second-hand cars, washing machines and so on which frequently break down, are expensive to repair and do not give long or continuous service.

They cannot afford the facilities that would allow them to go to work (especially transport and baby minders).

The welfare benefit system works in such a way that if someone in poverty gets an

Figure 4.8 The cycle of
deprivation

Source: Holman
(1978), p. 117

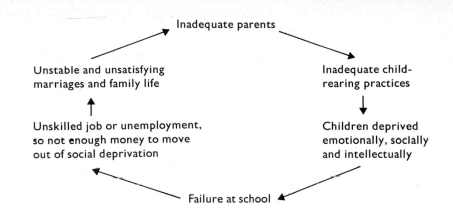

increase in income (say by getting a better-paid job) the benefits they are entitled
to are reduced so they end up no better off.

*Devise other illustrations to demonstrate the viciously circular nature of poverty.
Try illustrating the virtuous circle of wealth too.*

In addition to these factors there are longer-term 'traps' which mean that the
children of those in poverty will also be caught. These include:

the lack of books in the home, which means that poor children are disadvantaged
compared to the children of the better off;

lack of study facilities in small, overcrowded homes;

schools in poor areas that tend to be old, lacking in facilities and unpopular with
teachers, the best of whom will go elsewhere;

stereotypes of children from poor homes, which mean that they are often treated as
failures in the first place. As a result they often do fail.

This approach explains why the children of the poor are also disproportionately likely
to be poor themselves in later life, despite the fact that their parents may try their
best for them. Clearly, this different diagnosis of why poverty may be inherited calls
for very different treatment from the New Right model.

According to the Social Democratic model:

Who or what is to blame for the existence of poverty?
What needs to be done to abolish it?
Has anything like this been done so far?

Marxists

For Marxists poverty is an inevitable consequence of capitalism. In the capitalist
system the wealth of the few is founded upon (and necessitates) the poverty of the
many. Marxists very much agree with the old aphorism; 'The rich get richer and the
poor get poorer' – the rich are getting richer *because* the poor are getting poorer.

The flow of resources from the many to the few works like this, according to
Marxists:

Those in work receive less for their labour than the value they create. This is the source of profit for the capitalist and dividends on shares for shareholders. Goods are always sold for more than the cost of producing them, including the wages of the workers. This will inevitably mean that ordinary workers as a group can never afford all the goods that are available to them – there will be over-production but under-consumption of goods. This is an internal contradiction in capitalism which cannot be resolved, according to Marx.

Capitalists compete among themselves to make the most profit by selling their goods to the highest number of consumers at the highest price and lowest production cost possible. Consumers are poor (as we just saw) and limited in number. Only production costs are easily altered. To cut these the capitalists will:

– pay the lowest wages possible (by attacking unions, etc.);

– introduce automated production processes.

The first means that those in work become even poorer. The second means that there will be a large number of people out of work, replaced by machines.

Those out of work (the 'reserve army of labour') will only be looked after because they may be needed again by the capitalists if new markets are found or if the old market for their goods picks up again. Within capitalism the Welfare State can and should do no more than this. It is the role of the Welfare State to keep the poor 'ticking over'. To waste any more than the minimum resources on them would:

– threaten profitability (because taxes on profits would increase);

– make the country uncompetitive with other capitalist systems abroad. The government would be wasting resources paying to keep the unemployed and paying higher wages which would put the price of goods up. Meanwhile competing capitalist countries are investing their resources in new and better technology while paying minimum wages and not bothering with such niceties as a Welfare State.

From the Marxist perspective, then, it is the structure of capitalism that causes poverty. A system which allows, even encourages, great wealth necessarily creates great poverty. The Marxist would argue that the development of what has been called the 'two nations' in Britain is a consequence of the fact that the government is the ruling committee of the capitalist class. People (predominantly in the North) without work and the hope of getting it, dependent on declining health and welfare services and benefits, are living in a very different world from those (predominantly in the South) in highly paid jobs receiving the benefits of tax cuts and other government measures and who do not use or need the Welfare State. The result has been and will continue to be riots in the principal sites of poverty, particularly the inner cities, as those marginalised by the system take matters into their own hands.

According to the Marxist model:

Who or what is to blame for the existence of poverty?
What needs to be done to abolish it?
Has anything like this been done so far?

Other conflict perspectives

Many writers on the subject would agree with the Marxists that poverty results from the conflict over scarce resources between groups in society. However, it is often argued that these groups are more specific and numerous than simply two main classes. Peter Townsend advances such a point of view. Adopting a position close to the Weberian perspective (which sees society as divided into numerous groups with different levels of status, power and marketable skills and knowledge), Townsend argues:

> 'There are elaborate rules of professional associations and trade unions, as well as of private firms and public services, including employment agencies and educational institutions, which control access of numbers and social characteristics of individuals . . . The form taken by the hierarchy of occupational classes, the differentiated work conditions, status and fringe benefits as well as earnings of those classes, and the institutions controlling access to different levels and sanctioning the conditions associated with each stratum, must comprise a major part of any explanation of poverty.'
> (Townsend 1979, pp. 918–19)

In addition to the different positions within the occupational hierarchy, and differences in the extent of power that a group can deploy to maintain and improve its life chances compared to other groups, there are also people who fall outside this hierarchy. These are 'dependants' (children and housewives, for example) who will either have no income (as in the case of some married women) or very low levels of state income. It is likely that not only will these dependants be in poverty, but people within the occupational hierarchy with a large number of dependants will be poor too.

Other groups are neither employed nor dependants. These people, the retired living alone or in pairs with no private income, the chronically sick, long-term unemployed, single-parent families and so on, are particularly likely to be in poverty. They have very few marketable skills or knowledge and very little power or status. In the conflict over scarce resources they will be the losers.

Townsend (1979) offers a six-point solution to this situation:

1 abolition of excessive wealth (through state policy to restrict it to a maximum permissible level)

2 abolition of excessive income (by state action to determine top levels of salary)

3 introducing a more equal income structure and the payment of incomes to dependants to abolish the distinction between earners and dependants

4 abolition of unemployment through a legally enforceable right to work

5 restrictions on the power and rewards of professions, greater public ownership, more industrial democracy and stress on co-operation rather than competition at work and in society

6 more community care for those in need of support so that individuals recognise their responsibilities to others in society.

What is your response to these suggestions?

Figure 4.9 The ingredients
of wealth

Source: Stark (1988)

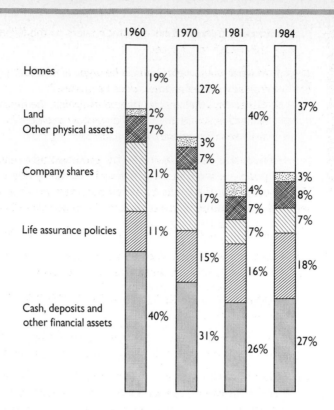

Functionalists

For the functionalists Townsend's proposals are a recipe for disaster. To writers such as Talcott Parsons (1952), Kingsley Davis and Wilbert Moore (1969) and Herbert Gans (1973) it is both inevitable and functional to have very steep gradients in income and wealth with, at the bottom, a reasonably substantial number of poor people.

A steep gradient in rewards is inevitable, according to these writers:

Everybody is born different, some able to do particular things better than others. Some are stronger, others more intelligent, others craftier. Some are good at business, others are good at the arts, and so on.

Every society considers some abilities good, others less good. This will differ from society to society, but whatever the valued qualities are, they will be rewarded.

Therefore, those lucky enough (say) to be born strong and healthy into a society which values physical strength will find themselves successful and rewarded in it.

It is also functional:

Though people are born with different potential abilities, these need to be developed.

To encourage people to go through the effort and temporary deprivation of doing this (for example, by going to university) there needs to be a high potential reward at the end.

Therefore the higher salaries and fringe benefits attached to the most difficult and most important occupations attract the people with the talent to do them well

Figure 4.10 Richard Branson, head of the Virgin 'empire' with personal holdings worth millions of pounds – a classic self-made entrepreneur

and encourage them to develop their talent to the full in order to ensure that they are chosen for the job.

1 *In what ways might Branson be atypical of wealthy people in the UK? What 'socially valued abilities' does he possess?*
2 *Generally, what are the arguments against the functionalist view?*
3 *According to the functionalist view, what would be the result of implementing Townsend's proposals 1, 2, 3 and 5?*

Functionalists believe it is inevitable that there will be a reasonably substantial number of poor people at the bottom of the social hierarchy because some people will be born without any of the talents society considers valuable or perhaps without the self-discipline required to develop them. Such people will not be rewarded.

The existence of poverty is functional for the following reasons:

It ensures that the dirty, dead-end jobs are done (since the poor have no choice other than to take these jobs if they wish to work).

It provides jobs for the middle class such as police, probation officers, social workers, psychiatrists and so on.

It reassures the rest of society by providing an example – 'At least I'm not like them' – and affirms the value of thrift, hard work, honesty and a stable family life.

It ensures that shoddy or second-hand goods find a market and that bad or poorly trained professionals can find employment (since the poor have to put up with teachers and doctors who cannot find employment elsewhere).

It increases social solidarity among the non-poor by providing a focus for charitable efforts, or (more negatively) providing a folk devil (e.g. itinerants).

It both sets the limits of and legitimates social norms by providing an example of social situations which are beyond them.

1 *According to the functionalist model:*

Who or what is to blame for the existence of poverty?
What needs to be done to abolish it?
Has anything like this been done so far?

2 *Divide into groups of about five. You are a policy review committee of a political party (either an established or a new one). Your tasks are:*

• *to formulate in writing your general philosophy on poverty in society;*

• *to decide specific policies for the party manifesto.*

Examination questions

Assess the argument that, rather than eliminating poverty, the Welfare State has created a form of 'dependency culture'.

AEB A-level, June 1992, Paper 2, question 6

'The Welfare State has blunted the extremes of poverty, but has failed to achieve its goal of eliminating it.' Explain and assess this view.

AEB A- level, June 1993, Paper 2, question 6

A skeleton answer for this question can be found on p. 146

Bibliography

Abel-Smith, B. and Townsend, P. (1965) *The Poor and the Poorest,* London: Bell

Alcock, P. (1987) *Poverty and State Support,* London: Longman

Barclay, P. *et al.* (1995) *Joseph Rowntree Foundation Inquiry into Income and Wealth,* London: Joseph Rowntree Foundation

Davis, K. and Moore, W. E. (1969) 'Some principles of stratification', in R. Bendix and S. M. Lipset (eds) *Class, Status and Power,* London: Routledge

Galbraith, K. (1962) *The Affluent Society,* Edinburgh: Hamish Hamilton

Gans, H. (1973) 'The positive functions of poverty', *American Journal of Sociology,* Vol. 78, No. 2

Gosling, A. *et al.* (1994) *What Has Happened to Wages?* London: Institute for Fiscal Studies

Holman, R. (1978) *Poverty: Explanations of Social Deprivation,* London: Martin Robinson

Kumar, V. (1993) *Poverty and Inequality in the UK: The Effects on Children,* London: National Children's Bureau

Lewis, O. (1964) *The Children of Sanchez,* Harmondsworth: Penguin,

Mack, J. and Lansley, S. (1985) *Poor Britain,* London: Unwin Hyman

McGregor, S. (1981) *The Politics of Poverty,* London: Longman

Miller, W. (1962) 'Lower class culture as a generating milieu of gang delinquency', in M. E. Wolfgang *et al.* (eds) *The Sociology of Crime and Delinquency,* New York: Wiley

Murray, C. (1984) *Losing Ground,* New York: Basic Books

Rentoul, J. (1987) *The Rich Get Richer,* London: Unwin Hyman

Parsons, T. (1952) *The Social System,* London: Routledge

Runciman, W. G. (1969) *Relative Deprivation and Social Justice,* Cambridge: Cambridge University Press

School for Advanced Urban Studies (1993) *People and Places: A 1991 Census Atlas of England,* Bristol: SAUS Publications (available from School for Advanced Urban Studies, Rodney Lodge, Grange Rd, Bristol, BS8 4EA)

Select Committee on Social Services (1988) *Poverty in the UK,* London: HMSO

Stark, T. A. (1988) *The New A–Z of Income and Wealth,* London: Fabian Society

Townsend, P. (1979) *Poverty in the United Kingdom,* Harmondsworth: Penguin

Walker, A. and Walker, C. (1987) *The Growing Divide,* London: Child Poverty Action Group

Wilkinson, C. (1995) *The Drop Out Society,* Leicester: National Youth Agency

Useful addresses

The Child Poverty Action Group publishes regular pamphlets on aspects of poverty. These are available from: 4th floor, 1–5 Bath St, London EC1V 9PY (Tel: 0171 253 3406).

National Youth Agency, 17–23 Albion Street, Leicester, LE1 6GD.

You can find numerous useful sites dealing with poverty issues on the World Wide Web. In 1995 there were four pages of sites, with links to other information. The current list of sites can be found using 'savvysearch'. Just go to the following address:

http://www.cs.colostate.edu/~dreiling/smartform.html

Then type in the word 'poverty' where it asks for the keyword/s to search for.

Answers to question 3 on p. 58.

a False

b True

c True (on any definition of 'rich')

d Impossible to say without defining 'poor' and knowing something about the distribution of wealth within the poorest 50 per cent.

e 'did better' is a bit vague. Generally, though, it seems as if the merely 'well off' did better than the 'very well off'.

Answer to question 2, p. 52.

Table 4.7 The public's perception of necessities

Standard-of-living items in rank order	% classing item as necessity	Standard-of-living items in rank order	% classing item as necessity
1. Heating to warm living areas of the home if it's cold	97	19. A hobby or leisure activity	64
2. Indoor toilet (not shared with another household)	96	20. Two hot meals a day (for adults)	64
3. Damp-free home	96	21. Meat or fish every other day	63
4. Bath (not shared with another household)	94	22. Presents for friends or family once a year	63
5. Beds for everyone in the household	94	23. A holiday away from home for one week a year, not with relatives	63
6. Public transport for one's needs	88	24. Leisure equipment for children, eg sports equipment or a bicycle*	57
7. A warm waterproof coat	87	25. A garden	55
8. Three meals a day for children*	82	26. A television	51
9. Self-contained accommodation	79	27. A 'best outfit' for special occasions	48
10. Two pairs of all-weather shoes	82	28. A telephone	43
11. Enough bedrooms for every child over 10 of different sex to have his/her own*	77	29. An outing for children once a week*	40
12. Refrigerator	77	30. A dressing gown	38
13. Toys for children*	71	31. Children's friends round for tea/a snack once a fortnight*	37
14. Carpets in living rooms and bedrooms	70	32. A night out once a fortnight (adults)	36
15. Celebrations on special occasions such as Christmas	69	33. Friends/family round for a meal once a month	32
16. A roast meat joint or its equivalent once a week	67	34. A car	22
17. A washing machine	67	35. A packet of cigarettes every other day	14
18. New, not second-hand, clothes	64		

*For families with children only

Source: Mack and Lansley (1985), p. 54

Health trends and social class in Britain

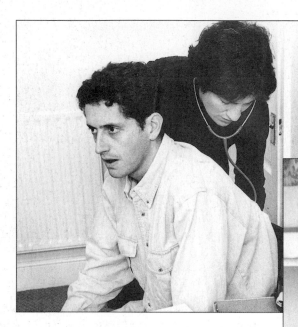

Figure 5.1 Unemployed men, mainly from social class V, have a 20 per cent higher death rate than employed men

The chances of survival for babies and young children are conditioned by the ethnic background of the mother. In the UK 3,500 children a year would not die if the infant mortality rate of social class V was that of social class I

This chapter is about the patterns of health in Britain. It will first examine trends in health and illness across the country as a whole, and then focus on the class structure to examine health inequalities as they are today and the trends over time. Finally it will look at various explanations that have been offered to account for these inequalities.

Health trends

The good news

The good news about the health of the British population is that generally it is improving over time. This is reflected in many of the the figures on health that we have access to:

Table 5.1 Death rates by occupation

Occupation unit	Direct age-standardized death rate per 100,000	
University teachers	287	
Physiotherapists	287	
Local authority senior officers	342	57
Company secretaries and registrars	362	60
Ministers, senior government officials, MPs	371	61
Office managers	377	64
School teachers	396	66
Architects, town planners	443	74
Civil servants, executive officers	467	78
Medical practitioners	494	81
Coal miners (underground)	822	141
Leather product makers	895	147
Machine tool operators	934	156
Coal miners (above ground)	972	160
Steel erectors, riggers	992	164
Fishermen	1,028	171
Labourers and unskilled workers, all industries	1,247	201
Policemen	1,270	209
Deck and engine room ratings	1,385	233
Bricklayers, labourers	1,644	274

SMR is Standardised Mortality Ratio. Figures in the column below 100 indicate a below-average mortality rate and those above 100 an above-average rate.

Source: Adapted from Townsend and Davidson (1988), Table 42

The infant mortality rate, thought to be a good indicator of the health of the population as a whole, has fallen from 14.7 in 1975 to 6.5 in 1993.

Life expectancy has increased. In 1901 a newborn baby boy could expect to live for 48 years, a girl for 52. By 1992 these figures had increased to 73.6 and 79 respectively.

Certain diseases have been virtually eradicated. These are primarily diseases that are amenable to treatment by immunisation programmes and responsive to improvements in hygiene. They include tuberculosis, typhoid, cholera, diphtheria, meningitis, polio and smallpox. While about 1 in every 350 people would die each year from tuberculosis in the 1850s, today the figure is 1 in 100,000. Cholera claimed 1 in every 550 each year in those days; today it has been wiped out in Britain.

Pregnancy and childbirth, which in the past were relatively dangerous, now produce few deaths – only 27 in 1993.

It is often thought that it was primarily medical advances such as immunisation that led to the improved health and decreased death rate that was a feature of the nineteenth and twentieth centuries in Britain. However, Thomas McKeown (1979) has suggested that the following were far more important (they are in the order of importance he gives them):

improved nutrition (resulting from agricultural improvements);

improvements in hygiene (resulting from better food and water purification, improved sewage disposal, better sterilisation and transport of milk);

improved environmental conditions (which came later), including improvements in living and working conditions, control of pollution and so on;

reduced birth rate which restricted numbers so that health improvements could be consolidated.

> 'In 1906 Albert Calnette and Camille Guérin discovered a vaccine against the TB germ – it became known as the BCG vaccine . . . Vaccines are made from the germs which cause the disease. Once a person has been vaccinated, the body builds up an immunity against these germs and will not catch the disease. Anti-toxins also help fight disease . . . When injected into a patient [they] help cure the disease.'

Figure 5.2

Source: Hartley (1988)

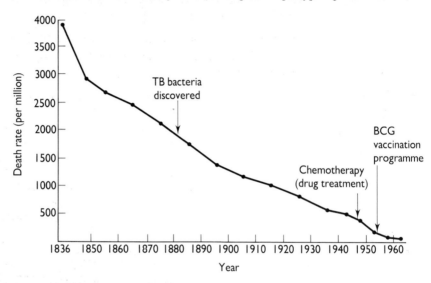

What does Figure 5.2 tell us about the significance of the BCG vaccination programme?

The bad news

The bad news is that the incidence of certain types of disease is on the increase in Britain. These include:

cancers of certain types. The death rates in cancer of the oesophagus, skin (malignant melanoma) and prostate (in men) increased considerably between 1971 and 1993 – from 84 to 137 for men and 91 to 121 for women in cancer of the oesophagus, for example, using the 1980–82 figure as the base of 100. Between 1979 and 1993 the number of deaths from all cancers rose from nearly 130,000 per year to 142,446.

mental disorder. Between 1979 and 1983 deaths associated with mental disorder increased from 3,211 to 4,142 per year).

diabetes. Deaths increased from almost 5,000 in 1979 to nearly 6,500 in 1984.

cardiovascular disease, from which the death toll has increased dramatically since the nineteenth century, so that today the death rate from heart attacks and strokes in Britain is more than five times higher than it was 100 years ago.

long-standing illness and *illness which limits activity,* in both the short and the long term, which is being reported by an ever-increasing percentage of the population. (34 per cent of the population reported long-standing illness in 1993 compared with 32 per cent in 1992).

the degenerative diseases (those associated with ageing), which are on the increase because the number of old people in the population is increasing.

diseases associated with HIV and AIDS. In 1993 over 2,000 new cases of AIDS were diagnosed. The figures represent patterns of transmission some years ago because of the long incubation period of the HIV virus. By September 1994 a total of 9,900 AIDS cases had been reported and 6,700 deaths were known to have occurred due to AIDS in the UK. Females represented only 8 per cent of cases and 7 per cent of deaths.

tuberculosis, which is reappearing in significant numbers among the disadvantaged in society. One in 50 people living in hostels or using day centres was suffering from TB in winter 1994.

Figure 5.3 AIDS: new cases per year in England and Wales, by exposure category (thousands)

Source: Social Trends 25 (1995)

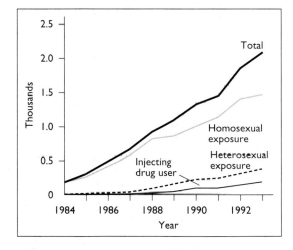

Overall life expectancies for men and women aged 15–44 years began to fall in the mid-1980s.

'Now there's a cancer to blame on the gays.
It's brutal and fatal and slowly invades.
The Moral Majority like it a lot
'Cause it's the wages of sin and the judgement of God.'
(Tom Robinson, 'Glad to be Gay', 1987 version © EMI)

Put this point into academic language. Use any or all of the following terms: social control, deviance, moral panic, hegemony, folk devils, control culture. Cohen (1980) and Hall (1978) should help to clarify these terms, as should a dictionary of sociology.

One fear for the long term is that the tools medicine uses against disease will no longer work. Antibiotics are one of medicine's success stories, yet they are a victim of their own success. Over time strains of organisms develop that are resistant to antibiotics and are more virulent than previous strains. By providing an environment in which only the strongest organisms can survive, medicine has unwittingly strengthened its 'enemy'. Researchers constantly attempt to develop new types of antibiotics, but these in turn begin to lose their effectiveness, and the number of possible types is not infinite. Doctors are worried that this battle will eventually be lost and that in the future infections will no longer be treatable as they are today.

One particularly virulent strain of 'germ' is methicillin-resistant staphylococcus aureus (MRSA or 'Super Staph'). By 1988 it had been identified in 99 hospitals around Britain and was particularly prevalent in the South East. It is susceptible to only one antibiotic, Vancomycin, which is expensive and toxic. Hospitals are a particularly congenial environment for Super Staph because the widespread use of antibiotics kills off other 'germs' and allow Super Staph to proliferate. It is not known how many deaths it has caused, but the elderly and ill are particularly prone to becoming infected with it.

Health and class: more bad news

More disturbing, perhaps, than the failure of medicine to fight some organisms and some sorts of disease is the fact that some groups in the population, particularly the working class, suffer much worse health than others. Such groups are missing the potential for better health. Let us look at some of the figures.

We should not be surprised to find that there are differences in the health and death statistics for the social classes as officially defined. The Registrar General's scheme of social class (Table 5.2), which is based on occupation, was created in order to allow the government to measure differences in the health of different groups in the population.

Table 5.2 The Registrar General's scheme of social class

Social class	Description	Examples	Percentage of economically active and retired males, 1986
I	Professional	Accountant Doctor Lawyer	5
II	Intermediate	Manager School teacher Nurse	18
IIIN	Skilled non-manual	Clerical worker Secretary Shop assistant	12
IIIM	Skilled manual	Bus driver Coal-face worker Carpenter	38
IV	Partly skilled	Agricultural worker Bus conductor Postman	18
V	Unskilled	Labourer Cleaner Dock worker	9

What problems can you see with the Registrar General's scale as a description of the the British class structure? (There are lots of problems.)

We will first examine morbidity (ill-health) and then mortality (death) across the class structure.

Morbidity

As we noted earlier, accurate statistics on morbidity are difficult to come by and are most easily collated from those on mortality. However, looking at the evidence from a variety of sources, including mortality statistics, the British Heart Survey and the OPCS longitudinal study, we can draw the following conclusions:

In 65 out of 78 categories of disease in men, the statistics show the sort of pattern depicted in Figure 5.4.

Figure 5.4

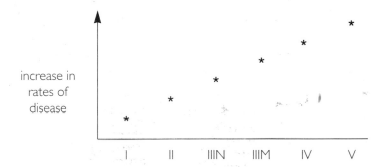

In men there is only one category, malignant melanoma (skin cancer caused by too much sunbathing), in which the pattern is reversed. However, particular professions suffer from particular diseases – for instance, male doctors tend to suffer more than average from drink-related diseases, as do journalists.

In women this pattern applies in 62 out of 82 categories of disease, with only four showing the reverse (three types of cancer and malignant melanoma), and the rest are evenly spread across the class structure.

Individuals in class V and those who are long-term unemployed have higher blood pressure and tend to be fatter than their class I counterparts. They are more likely to suffer from arthritis, haemorrhoids, angina, respiratory problems and deafness. They are more prone to alcohol-related diseases and mental illness (though for women being a housewife is more likely to be associated with mental illness than being long-term unemployed). If members of the working class get cancer they are less likely to survive it.

Children of poor families have more bad teeth and bad lungs than those in more affluent ones. Respiratory disease and accidents are the most highly class-related causes of death in children. Children in social classes IV and V are between five and seven times more likely to die from accidents involving fire, falling, drowning or being hit by a motor car than are children from social class I, so we can assume that accident-related injuries are also closely correlated with class. Children living in deprived districts of Glasgow were found to be nine times more likely to be admitted to hospital than children in non-deprived districts of that city.

The so-called 'executive diseases' (coronary heart disease, strokes and peptic ulcers) are now more common in the manual working class than among the executives of classes I and II. However, the 'diseases of poverty' (such as cancer of the cervix and tuberculosis) really are concentrated among the poor and seem likely to remain so.

Lower social classes tend to have children with lower birth weight and shorter stature than those of higher social groups. These inequalities seem to continue into adulthood – for example, men in the top grades of the civil service are on average 5 cm taller than those in the lowest grades.

It is estimated that by the end of the century there would be 100,000 fewer chronically sick and disabled people if health inequalities between social classes were reduced by only 25 per cent.

Asians living in Britain are more likely to suffer diabetes and coronary heart disease than the white population. Psychiatric illness appears to be more common among Afro-Carribeans living in Britain than among the population as a whole.

Mortality

3,500 children a year would not die if the Infant Mortality Rate of social class V was the same as that of social class I.

A reduction of 25 per cent in the health inequalities between social classes would produce 20,000 fewer deaths a year in people under pension age in the manual classes.

Unemployed men and their wives, most of whom come from social class V, have a 20 per cent higher death rate than employed men. Unemployed men are 493 per cent more likely to suffer death related to mental disorders, 503 per cent more likely to die of kidney diseases and 628 per cent more of 'congenital anomalies' than the national average. Their suicide rate is 173 per cent higher.

Social class V suffer more from the four biggest killers in Britain than do the higher social groups. These are heart disease, stroke, lung cancer and stomach ulcer.

The Standardised Mortality Ratio (see box on next page) for males between 15 and 65 is double in social class V what it is in social class I (around 120 compared to around 60).

The chances of survival of foetuses and babies continue to be conditioned by the ethnic background of the mother, as Figure 5.5 shows.

Mortality rates from strokes and hypertension are very high among African and Caribbean immigrants, while Asians are more likely than whites to die of coronary heart attacks. Ethnic origin is, of course, related to social class in that most immigrants find themselves in the lower part of the class structure.

To sum up, we can say that the lower social classes are more likely to suffer from nearly all the major diseases than the higher social classes, and they are more likely to go to an early grave.

Figure 5.5 Infant, perinatal, neonatal and post-neonatal mortality by mother's country of birth, 1982–5, England and Wales

Source: Taylor and Field (1993)

Infant mortality: deaths to infants under one year of age per thousand live births. Perinatal mortality: stillbirths and deaths in the first week of life per thousand total live and still births. Neonatal mortality: deaths in the first 28 days of life per thousand live births. Postneonatal mortality: deaths at ages over 28 days and under one year per thousand live births.

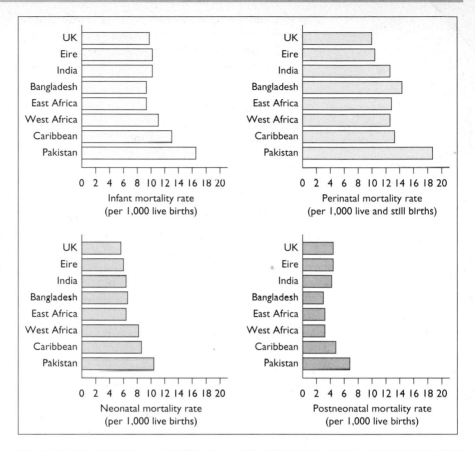

The Standardised Mortality Ratio shows the relative chances of death for a given age. The average SMR for the population as a whole for that age is 100; an SMR below this indicates greater 'survivability'.

The trends

Between the early 1970s and the early 1980s deaths from all causes dropped from an SMR of 100 to 80 for non-manual classes. Among the manual classes it only declined from 130 to 120.

In the same decade deaths from certain diseases, including lung cancer (especially for women) and coronary heart disease, dropped sharply among the non-manual classes but only fell slightly or even increased for the manual classes.

The health gap between the social classes is widening as the health of social class I improves at a faster rate than social class V. For example, between 1971 and 1981 there was a 15 per cent overall decline in deaths from heart disease, but for men and women in non-manual occupations there was only a 1 per cent decrease.

The only exception to the generally widening gap in health between the social classes is that class differences in deaths of babies aged between one month and one year narrowed considerably between 1971 and 1981. There was also a small reduction in differentials between 1 and 4 years (especially for girls).

The class differential in maternal mortality has remained about the same in recent years.

Between the end of the 1950s and the beginning of the 1980s there was a decline in the death rate in classes I and II of 37 per cent for men aged between 45 and 54 years. For men in classes IV and V of that age the decline was only 7 per cent.

The number of people with long-standing illness in the various classes increased between 1974 and 1984. This increase was most marked in the lower social classes, so here again the gap has been widening.

More recent detailed figures are available for Northern England (Phillimore and Beattie 1994). During the decade 1981–91 'the poorest areas have increasingly come adrift from the remainder of the population in their mortality experience . . . on almost every criterion of health available for the study, differentials [between the affluent and the deprived] are widening, not narrowing'.

Generally, then, we can say that all classes have profited from a decline in the death rate, but higher-status groups have profited the most. However, in the case of certain diseases and long-standing (chronic) illness, there has been an increase in incidence. Here again the lower social groups have borne the brunt of the increase.

Before going on to read the following sections, brainstorm as many reasons as you can to explain the higher mortality and morbidity rates in the lower social classes.

The official response to the statistics on class inequalities

A report on inequalities in health was commissioned by the Labour government in the late 1970s, and Sir Douglas Black was appointed to head the inquiry. When the Black Report was published in August 1980 the Conservative government gave it only limited circulation (250 copies) – and that only after a year's delay. In the foreword to the Penguin edition of the Black Report the then Secretary of State for Social Services stated that he considered implementation of the report's recommendations too expensive and probably ineffective.

An update of the Black Report, entitled *The Health Divide,* was published in March 1987. As had happened with the earlier report, it was starved of publicity: at the last minute the Health Education Council chair, Sir Brian Bailey, prevented the Council from holding a press conference to launch the report, and on 1 April the Council was abolished and replaced by the Health Education Authority, with Sir Brian as its chair.

Explanations for inequalities in health

The structural–material explanation

This approach points to factors such as the following to explain the poorer health of the working class:

insufficient household income (leading to poor diet, etc.);

unsafe, overcrowded and polluted homes;

cold, damp and unhygenic conditions in the home;

poor communication with the outside world and help agencies;

lack of knowledge and skills in, for example, baby care;

types of working conditions in which accidents are likely;

exposure to hazardous materials at work;

work that is physically and mentally exhausting;

the greater likelihood of severe life events occurring which will then affect health (deaths, poor relationships, etc.);

smoking and drinking caused by stress, worry and depression resulting from all the above;

the operation of the 'inverse care law', which states that 'the availability of good medical care tends to vary inversely with the need for it in the population served' (Dr J. Tudor Hart 1971).

Give specific examples to illustrate how each of the above could lead to disease. How could you test whether they are really a cause of greater ill-health?

We will examine the last point regarding the 'inverse care law' in some detail. The lack of availability manifests itself in three ways: geographically, in terms of knowledge about facilities, and in the treatment received.

Figure 5.6 Beveridge's 'giant evil', squalor, is still with us, as illustrated by this damp council flat in London.

Geographical inequalities

Areas where working-class people are most numerous tend to be provided with the fewest and worst health facilities, as Figure 5.7 shows. This is despite the fact that working-class people suffer worse health than the middle class, so they should have more and better facilities. Hart (1971) identifies the following reasons for this state of affairs:

Industrial and mining areas have traditionally been serviced by low-status general practitioners, not specialists, hospitals and so on.

Doctors 'most able to choose where they will work go to middle class areas and . . . the areas with highest mortality and morbidity tend to get those doctors who are least able to choose where they will work'. This is partly because 'the better-endowed, better-equipped, better-staffed areas of the service draw to themselves more and better staff, and more and better equipment, and their superiority is compounded'.

'The career structure and traditions of our medical schools make it clear that time spent at the periphery in the hospital service, or at the bottom of the heap in industrial general practice, is almost certain disqualification for further advancement.'

Figure 5.7 Vital statistics: Regional Health Authority areas in England, 1993

Source: Adapted from *The Compendium of Health Statistics 1993*, London: Office of Health Economics

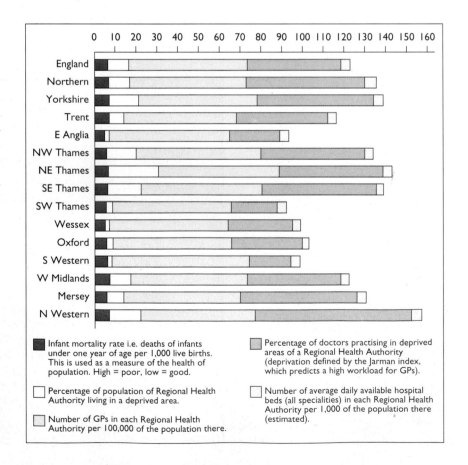

1 *Which Regional Health Authority had the fewest:*
   hospital beds
   general practitioners
   as a proportion of its population?

2 *Which RHA had the lowest percentage of GPs operating in deprived areas as*
   a proportion of its population living there?

3 *On the basis of these data, which RHA overall would you say is the most in*
   need of additional health resources?

4 *What other quantifiable measures of resource deprivation could be used to*
   compare RHAs?

Inequalities in knowledge

People in different social classes behave differently in the medical environment because of the different levels of knowledge they have about it. Those who understand the nature of illnesses, pregnancy and birth control, the facilities available and the procedures for utilising them, will get better service than those who lack such knowledge. Surveys show that middle-class people score more highly on questions testing this sort of knowledge than working-class people do. Similarly, middle-class people are more likely to be critical of deficiencies in medical service and to demand changes and more information than working-class people are.

It has been suggested that the different social classes *perceive* health facilities in the same way, but members of the working class are more diffident about expressing their views: 'Patients in the professional class were more likely to ask questions, while those in the unskilled manual group more often waited to be told' (Cartwright and O'Brien 1978). Middle-class people are especially able to use this knowledge to take advantage of facilities for preventive services. They therefore have a proactive rather than a reactive approach to health (that is, they tend to prevent health problems from arising rather than simply responding to them once they appear).

Recently sociologists have come under fire for making statements such as Cartwright and O'Brien's. It is suggested that, being middle class, sociologists are merely giving vent to their prejudices about the working class. Their studies and results are constructed and interpreted in such a way as to confirm these prejudices. Do you feel that this criticism is valid? How could you objectively test differences between the social classes in these respects?

Differential treatment by professionals

Doctors and other professionals behave differently when dealing with people from different social groups. Studies show that middle-class patients are given longer consultations by doctors – about six minutes compared to just over four and a half for the working class (see Table 5.3 on next page). More problems are discussed during the typical middle-class consultation (about four compared to about three) – though the ratio of 'social' as opposed to 'medical' problems is about the same for the two groups.

When working-class patients do ask questions, they are more likely to be cut short by the doctor than middle-class questioners are. Doctors are more likely to know the

Table 5.3 General practice consultations with middle-class and working-class patients aged 65 and over

	Middle Class	Working Class
Average length of consultation	6.2	4.7
Average number of questions asked by patient	3.7	3.0
Average number of problems discussed	4.1	2.8
Average number of symptoms mentioned to interviewer prior to consultation	2.2	3.0

Source: Patrick and Scambler (1986); adapted from Cartwright and O'Brien (1976)

names and domestic situations of their middle-class patients than their working-class ones, despite the fact that the latter are likely to have been with the practice longer.

Differential treatment is not only a matter of social class. Black patients have been found to talk more to a psychiatrist if they share the same ethnic background. White psychiatrists appear more likely to classify black patients as mentally disturbed than white patients. This is because, as Hart suggests, doctors are most frequently drawn from the ranks of the white middle class (and are often the children of doctors) so they find it difficult to empathise with other social groups.

Assuming we would want equality of opportunity for all social groups in the medical situation, what policies could we implement to bring this about? (Remember to cover each of the three categories of inequality discussed here – geography, knowledge and treatment by professionals.)

The artefact explanation – more good news?

An 'artefact' is something that is made by people – it is artificial rather than natural. This explanation says that the 'bad news' about class and health is not really true – it only appears to be the case because of artificial and inaccurate statistics. The statistics are wrong for these reasons:

The percentage of people in the lower social groups is declining all the time. Eventually there could be very few people in social class V, yet it would still be possible to talk about 'the health divide'. In reality, as this class disappears, so does the health divide.

Why are social classes IV and V disappearing?

Even for those who remain in the lower social groups the general level of health is improving. In some types of illness the rate of improvement is greater in the lower social groups than the higher. These facts should not be forgotten.

Arguments about the health divide are usually based on figures that relate only to males of working age. If females and older and younger people were taken into account many aspects of the divide would be shown to be artificial. For example, the higher social groups are more likely to suffer from the degenerative diseases that affect older people more (since higher social classes live longer and so have more older people among their number).

Organising the statistics in terms of 'social class', defined in terms of the job of the breadwinner in the family, is meaningless. There are many much more meaningful ways of classifying people and their diseases (for example by income, by ownership of assets, by social isolation, by overcrowding and so on). Therefore the results of such arbitrary classification are meaningless too.

 In reply to the last point, the authors of Inequalities in Health *(Townsend, Davidson and Whitehead 1988) argue that using social class defined in this way probably underestimates the degree of health inequalities, if anything. How would you reply to the other points?*

The social selection explanation

According to this argument, people in poor health tend to move to or stay in the bottom of the occupational scale or the ranks of the unemployed because of their poor health. It is not that they have poor health because they are in classes IV and V, rather they are in classes IV and V because of their poor health.

The fact that people at higher levels of the civil service are taller than their lower status colleagues is easily explained. Psychologists have shown that taller people get better jobs because people perceive them more positively than shorter ones. But you do not need to be a psychologist to realise that someone who is frequently ill and takes time off school or work is less likely to succeed than someone who is healthy and in full possession of their faculties during their period of education and at work.

 What sort of evidence would you need to collect in order to confirm or refute this idea?

The behavioural–cultural explanation

This explanation blames those with ill-health for not looking after themselves properly. The cause lies in unhealthy behaviour such as smoking and drinking too much, not taking enough exercise, eating the wrong sorts of foods and so on. Not only is the culprits' behaviour inclined to make them less healthy, they are less likely to bother to make use of the facilities provided to keep them healthy, for instance by going for medical check-ups, using family planning facilities and the rest. These habits are often transmitted across the generations in the process of socialisation and could therefore be said to be part of the 'culture of poverty' (see page 60).

Figure 5.8 'A few simple changes' in your behaviour can reduce your risk of heart disease, according to the behavioural–cultural point of view.

The heart of the matter

Coronary heart disease is the most common cause of death in Britain. Each year it kills about 170,000 men and women. This means that heart disease is the country's biggest random killer, causing more deaths than all the forms of cancer combined.

Heart disease has no single cause – it often results from a combination of factors – but take heart. There's so much the British Heart Foundation is already doing to fight back, and there's plenty that you can do to help us and to help yourself.

So you think heart disease will never happen to you? Let's take a closer look at your heart then...

TWEEK

Just look at the state of it! However, let's not panic, there's a lot you can do to reduce your risk of heart disease...

FLICK!

BE-BER BUMP! BA-BUMP! UMP!

We can get rid of this lot for a start. There, don't you feel better already?

British Heart Foundation
The heart research charity

A common problem you can fight with common sense and our help

Figure 5.9 Changing diet in
Britain (% change in
consumption, 1965–92)

*Source: Sociology
Update 1995*, p. 7

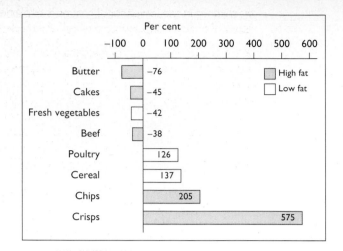

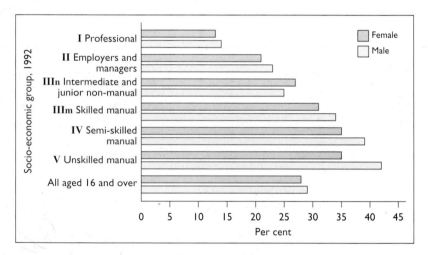

Figure 5.10 The
relationship between
smoking and employment

*Source: Social Trends
25 (1995)*, Table 7.21

In the autumn of 1986 the Under-Secretary of State for Health, Edwina Currie, declared that the real cause of the poorer health of Northerners was their diet. Ill-health could best be tackled by 'impressing upon people the need to look after themselves better'. Despite much criticism of her outspoken comments on this theme, she continued to expound her view: 'Don't eat the pud! There's no law that says you've got to eat everything that's under your nose' (advice given to businessmen and women, quoted in *Your Business*, July 1988).

Members of the lower social classes and the unemployed tend to smoke and drink more and to take less exercise – all causes of high cholesterol levels and heart problems, from which they suffer more than other groups. Low-income families eat more unhealthy food like processed meat and fried meals. They buy fewer fresh vegetables and healthy fibre-rich foods. They have larger families, too, which means greater danger of infection and fewer resources for each child.

Respiratory diseases in children have been shown to be highly related to parents' smoking, and the risk of infection increases with the size of the family. Thus the class-related nature of these illnesses can be explained by the patterns of behaviour of parents in lower social groups. Similarly the larger number of fatal accidents suffered by children in the lower social groups is explained by their greater carelessness, lower levels of parental supervision and general macho attitudes towards danger.

According to proponents of the behavioural–cultural explanation, the structural argument to the effect that the lower social groups are forced into certain forms of behaviour by their low income and poor environments is nonsense. You need to have money to smoke and drink. If class V followed the example of class I and moderated this behaviour they could afford to feed their children better (especially if they had fewer of them). Going for a regular two-mile walk in order to become fitter costs nothing, yet only 13 per cent of class V did it in 1983 compared to 30 per cent of class I. Indoor swimming costs very little, yet the figures were 3 per cent and 12 per cent respectively.

To test the cultural–behavioural explanation, develop a questionnaire concerning people's eating, drinking and smoking habits. Also, ask them about their attitudes to and knowledge of food and health (e.g. by setting them test questions about which are 'healthy' and 'unhealthy' foods). By asking them about their age, occupation and so on you can determine whether there is any correlation between these and the factors tested.

Figure 5.11 The way to create a healthier Britain? The HEA's attempt to change people's behaviour

Figure 5.12 Heading for an
early grave? Highly
stressed, and possibly a
smoker too

Stress

It has been argued that the lower social groups are more likely to suffer stress, and
this makes them more prone to disease. For example, people living in noisy and
dangerous environments who have stressful or insecure jobs will be at risk; so will
those whose jobs are boring, repetitive and never change. The British Medical
Association (BMA 1987) thinks stress may be a significant factor in accounting for the
worse health of black immigrants to Britain than that of the host population.

Studies into the effects of stress demonstrate that important events in a person's life
can provoke illnesses of various kinds, both physical and mental. For example,
bereavement, redundancy, retirement or the failure of one's plans have been shown
to be frequently followed by depressive illness or gastro-intestinal disease. The
mechanisms causing this are associated with the immune system (so that the person
cannot throw off disease), and elements of the nervous and chemical systems of the
body.

 *What methodology or methodologies could you employ to test the relationship
between stress and ill-health?*

Genetic differences

There is evidence that the lower social groups are genetically more prone to certain
types of disease and less resistant to others than the higher social groups. Research
by Beveridge Beardmore (1972) has shown them more likely to have blood group
O, though what the significance of this may be is not known. Asians in Britain have
higher levels of cardiovascular disease than is found in other groups, even though
typical Asian food is healthier in this respect than typical British food. The BMA thinks
genetic differences may underlie this otherwise puzzling finding. Another genetic
difference, this time in skin pigmentation, is surely the reason why white Australians
are extremely prone to skin cancer whereas Aborigines get it hardly at all.

1 *How might genetic differences between social classes in Britain arise? Do you consider this a likely explanation? Explain your answer.*

2 *Take each of the six explanations for the health divide and consider what social policies could be employed to narrow it.*

Examination questions

Critically examine the relationship between social class background and the nature and distribution of different types of illness.

AEB A-level, Summer 1994, Paper 2, question 5

A skeleton answer for this question can be found on p. 148.

'The Welfare State has still not significantly redistributed health resources in favour of the most needy.' Critically evaluate the sociological arguments for and against this view.

AEB A-level, June 1992, Paper 2, question 5

Outline and assess different sociological explanations of the continuation of social class inequalities in health and health care.

AEB A-level, June 1993, Paper 2, question 5

Bibliography

Baggott, R. (1994) *Health and Health Care in Britain,* New York: St Martin's Press

Beardmore, B. W. I. (1972) *Frontiers in Comparative Medicine,* Oxford: Oxford University Press

Black, N. (1984) *Health and Disease: A Reader,* Milton Keynes: Open University Press

British Medical Association (1987) *Deprivation and Ill-Health* (available from the BMA, Tavistock Square, London, WC1H 9JP; has a good bibliography)

Cartwright, A. and O'Brien, M. (1976) 'Social class variations in health care and in general practitioner consultations', in M. Stacey (ed.) *The Sociology of the NHS,* Sociological Review Monograph No. 22, Keele: University of Keele

—— (1978) 'Social class variations in health care and in the nature of general practice consultations', pp. 89–97 in D. Tuckett and J. M. Kaufert (eds) *Basic Readings in Medical Sociology* London: Tavistock

Cohen, S. (1980) *Folk Devils and Moral Panics,* New York: St Martin's Press

Doll, R. and Peto, R. (1981) *The Causes of Cancer,* Oxford: Oxford University Press

Gibson, I. (1981) *Class, Health and Profit,* Norwich: University of East Anglia

Green, J. and Miller, D. (1986) *AIDS: The Story of a Disease,* London: Grafton

Hall, S. (1978) *Policing the Crisis,* London: Macmillan

Hart, J. T. (1971) 'The inverse care law', *Lancet,* Vol. 1, pp. 405–12

Hart, N. (1985) *The Sociology of Health and Medicine,* Ormskirk: Causeway Press

Hartley, L. (1988) *The History of Medicine,* Oxford: Blackwell

Heller, T. (1977) *Poor Health, Rich Profits,* London: Spokesman

'It's the poor what get the disease', *New Scientist,* 7 August 1986

McKeown, T. (1979) *The Role of Medicine,* Oxford: Blackwell

Mitchell, J. (1984) *What Is To Be Done About Illness and Health?* Harmondsworth: Penguin

Office of Population Censuses and Surveys (1987) *The General Household Survey 1985,* London: HMSO

Patrick, D. L. and Scambler, G. (eds) (1986) *Sociology as Applied to Medicine,* 2nd edn, Edinburgh: Ballière Tindall

Phillimore, P. and Beattie, A. (1994) *Health and Inequality: The Northern Region 1981–1991,* Newcastle: University of Newcastle upon Tyne

Richman, J. (1987) *Medicine and Health,* London: Longman

Silverman, D. (1988) *Medical Sociology,* London: Sage

Taylor, S. and Field, D. (1993) *Sociology of Health and Health Care,* Oxford: Blackwell Science

Townsend, P., Davidson, N. and Whitehead, M. (1988) *Inequalities in Health,* 2nd edn, Harmondsworth: Penguin

6

Gender, health and welfare

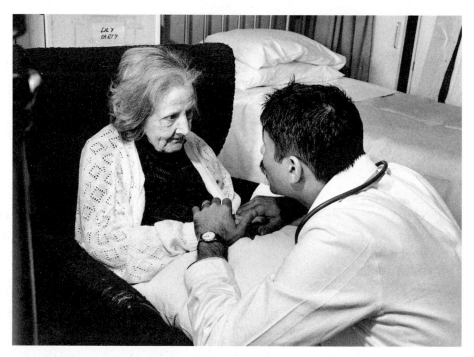

Figure 6.1

'*Women live longer but suffer from more health problems in their lifetime, and many of these problems are specific to the female gender.*'

Agnes Miles, Women, Health and Medicine

This chapter will first examine the evidence about and explanations of gender inequalities in health, both within the UK and abroad. It will then consider the role of women in health and welfare work.

Morbidity and mental illness

In 1993, 14 per cent of women compared to 12 per cent of men reported acute health problems (that is, illness or injury which restricted their activity in the two weeks prior to being interviewed). The gender differential widened to 3 per cent during the 1980s but has recently narrowed.

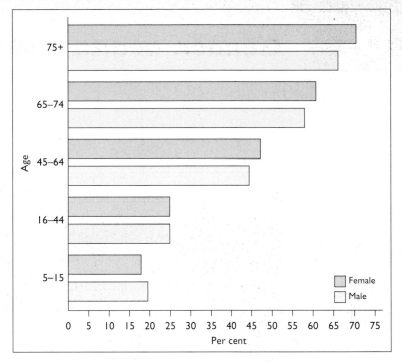

Figure 6.2 Respondents
reporting long-standing
illness, 1990 (Great Britain)

Source: Baggott (1994),
Figure 1.2, citing
OPCS (1992)

Chronic sickness (that is, a long-standing illness disability or infirmity) is higher for
women than men across almost the whole age range, as Figure 6.2 shows.

Of these, 18 per cent of men but 21 per cent of women reported their chronic
sickness to be so severe as to limit their activity.

Women see their doctor more frequently than men: 19 per cent of women
compared to 14 per cent of men had seen their GP in the fortnight before the
1993/4 General Household Survey. In 1992 women saw an NHS doctor six times
and men four times, on average.

In 1993/4, 13 per cent of females compared to 6 per cent of males had been a
patient in hospital in the previous 12 months.

Two thirds of the 4 million disabled people in the UK are women.

57 per cent of admissions to mental hospital for any disorder are women. However,
women are more likely than men to be admitted for certain types of mental
illness, particularly:

– emotional disturbance

– neurotic disorders

– depression

– senile dementia.

Men equal women in the number of admissions for schizophrenia and paranoia and
have a much greater admission rate for alcohol dependence.

One in five women suffer acute stress or depression, according to the government's advisory Women's National Commission. In July 1988 they reported that women are twice as likely to suffer severe stress as men because they tend to be 'the buffer and absorber of stresses of the other members of the family'. Women cope by turning stress in on themselves, and this often leads to alcohol or cigarette addiction. Women are more likely than men to become heavy and dependent drinkers following stressful events such as marital breakdown.

Mortality

Figure 6.3 Death rates (per 1,000 population) for people aged under 65, England and Wales, by gender and selected cause of death

Source: Social Trends 25, Figure 7.27

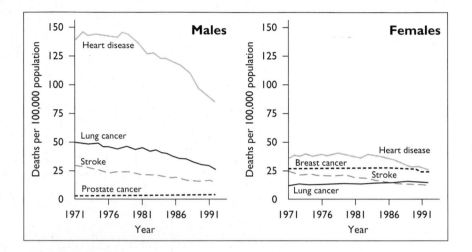

Look at Figure 6.3 What trends are shown by these data? What explanations might there be for them?

Life expectancy at birth in the UK was 79 years for females but 73.6 for males (1993).

As a result, around 70 per cent of those over 75 are women, and this percentage increases for older age groups.

The number of male babies who die before they are 28 days old is consistently greater than the number of female babies (1,603 compared to 1,192 in 1993). Though more male than female babies are born, this does not account for the greater number of male deaths. The rates of spontaneous abortion, miscarriage and stillbirth are also higher for boys than girls.

The infant mortality rate (IMR: deaths in the first year per 1,000 live births) for boys in the UK in 1993 was 7.8, whereas for girls it was 6.2. However, while the death rate (number of deaths per 1,000 live births) decreased for men from 12.6 to 11.1 between 1961 and 1993 it increased for women from 11.4 to 11.5.

The attentive student may notice an apparent paradox here: women suffer from worse health than men, yet they live longer! The possible explanations for how they manage to pull off this particular trick are:

Though women suffer more ill-health, the predominantly male forms of ill-health (such as emphysema and heart disease; see Tables 6.1 and 6.2) are more fatal.

Table 6.1 Patients consulting GPs, by gender and selected disease or condition, 1991–2

	Males	Females	All persons
Dermatitis and eczema	636	879	760
Asthma	429	422	425
Hypertension	357	479	419
Neurotic disorders	202	481	344
Ischaemic heart disease	204	137	170
Normal pregnancy	–	287	147
Migraine	58	169	115
Diabetes	119	102	111
Obesity	38	125	82
Cerebrovascular disease	64	68	66
Acute reaction to stress	18	35	26
Drug dependence	19	19	19
Breast cancer	–	30	15
Alcohol dependence	20	6	13
Lung cancer	9	5	7
Malignant melanoma of the skin	2	3	2
All diseases and conditions	6,999	8,575	7,803

Source: Social Trends 25, Table 7.12

Table 6.2 Hospital in-patient cases, by gender and main diagnosis, 1992–3

United Kingdom	Males	Percentages Females
Infectious and parasitic diseases	2	1
Neoplasms	11	11
Endocrine, nutritional, metabolic and immunity	2	2
Blood	1	2
Mental disorders	4	4
Nervous system and sense organs	6	7
Circulatory system	13	11
Respiratory system	9	7
Digestive system	13	12
Genito-urinary system	7	13
Skin	2	2
Musculo-skeletal and connective tissue	6	7
Congenital anomalies	2	1
Perinatal conditions	3	2
Signs and symptoms	9	10
Injury and poisoning	10	8
All diagnoses (excluding pregnancy) (thousands) (=100%)	4,207	4,502
Complications of pregnancy (thousands)	–	1,145
Other reasons for contact with health services (thousands)	455	556
All in-patient cases (thousands)	4,662	6,203

Source: Social Trends 25, Table 7.13

Men enjoy generally better health than women but are killed off by accidents and diseases to which they are more susceptible and which are often fatal.

Women suffer worse health precisely *because* they live longer – that is, they often suffer from the degenerative diseases associated with old age.

The statistics on morbidity or mortality or both are wrong or misleading in some way.

Statistics from abroad

Life expectancy at birth has increased dramatically (by over a third) in most developing countries. Twenty-three developing countries now have a life expectancy figure of over 70 years – comparable with the developed world. However, in many developing countries life expectancy is around 50, and in others such as Sierra Leone as low as 40 (1990 figures). The IMR, while generally lower in low-income economies, still favours females there. Women could expect to live longer than men in all but four of the 36 underdeveloped countries identified by the World Bank in 1984. Interestingly these four are close neighbours: India, Pakistan, Nepal and Bhutan.

What hypotheses can you formulate to explain the higher death rate of females in these four countries only? Think of at least three possible reasons. How could your hypotheses be tested:

given unlimited resources
given the resources you actually have?

In none of the other 92 countries above this level of development was there a higher life expectancy for men than for women. Only Iran had an equal life expectancy at birth for males and females (61 years).

The average life expectancy advantage females had over males (calculating from the time they were born) in 1984 was:

– one year in low-income economies

– four years in middle-income economies

– five years in upper-middle-income economies

– six years in industrial market economies.

Develop some hypotheses to explain these figures.

Comparing the gap between male and female life expectancies at birth in 1965 with that in 1984:

– the average for low-income countries had reduced by one year

– in middle-income countries it had increased by one year

– in upper-middle-income countries it had increased by one year

– in industrial market economies it had remained constant at six years.

In East European ex-socialist economies the gap between male and female life expectancy at birth was five years (66 years as against 71 years) in 1984. In none of the eight countries in this category was male expectancy greater than 69 years or female less than 74 years. The male/female life expectancy gap had reduced by two years between 1965 and 1984 in these countries.

Explaining the gender differences

In Chapter 5 we looked at the following explanations for the inequalities in health of the different social classes:

structural–material
artefact
social selection
behavioural–cultural
stress
genetic differences.

Try applying the same types of explanation (excluding the third, which does not apply here) to the inequalities in health of the sexes – the greater morbidity of some types among women and the higher mortality rates among men. Do this exercise before you read the following sections!

The structural–material explanation

Figure 6.4 Not at work ... or just not paid for working?

Women's position in society shapes their experience of health and health care. The health-threatening aspects of women's role in Western industrialised society include the following:

the burden of child care

the demands of looking after other people's health

the demands of domestic labour

poor employment conditions (low pay, insecure, part time)

greater exposure to poor housing

greater exposure to poverty.

The artefact explanation

According to this explanation, women do not really suffer worse health than men; however, the statistics only make it appear that they do for the following reasons:

Often the statistics only relate to one variable (in the present case, sex). This can be misleading. For example, women who are in low social classes and/or ethnic minorities are doubly disadvantaged in terms of health as well as in other ways. For instance, in 1985, 41 per cent of women in social class V were suffering from a long-standing illness; the average for all women, though, was 31 per cent. If age is taken into account too we find, for example, that social class V men between the ages of 45 and 64 years suffer more chronic illness than females of the same age group and social class. Thus the variables we choose, and those we omit, can alter what the statistics appear to show. As women are disproportionately represented in particular occupational categories and age groups, these may be the important factors, not sex.

The figures often do not tell us what we want to know. For example, do women visit the doctor more frequently than men because they are suffer more ill-health, or for some other reason?

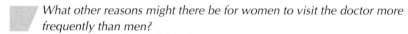 *What other reasons might there be for women to visit the doctor more frequently than men?*

Statistics based on surveys can be inaccurate because of high non-response rates and the practice of proxy reporting for men (i.e. wives fill in the form, even the sections relating to the man's health and medical history).

Statistics on morbidity are notoriously inaccurate because of the clinical iceberg. We cannot be sure about the facts of gender-related differences in morbidity because women may, for example, be more willing to adopt the sick role than men (or, conversely, be more inclined to 'soldier on'). Similarly self-report studies (e.g. the question 'Have you suffered incapacitating illness in the last 24 days?' asked by the General Household Survey) are also unreliable.

Examination question

Assess the arguments and evidence which suggest that women make greater use of health services than men.

AEB A-level, November 1993, Paper 12, question 5

The cultural–behavioural explanation

Those who reason in this way argue that men do things so seriously health-threatening that they are likely to die from them. For example, they eat the wrong foods, smoke more than women and drink more. Generally they are less aware of the condition of their bodies, the importance of balanced eating and so on.

Well over half the difference between the male and female death rate can be accounted for by differences in behaviour (for instance, cigarette smoking, alcohol consumption, occupational hazards, suicide and traffic accidents). Figures 6.5 and 6.6 illustrate alcohol and drug consumption by gender.

Figure 6.5 Consumption of alcohol above sensible levels, by gender and age, Great Britain, 1992 (percentages)

Source: Social Trends 25, Table 7.24

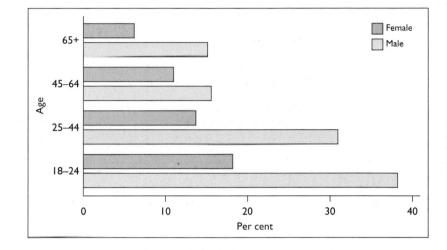

Figure 6.6 New drug users, by gender and age, Great Britain, 1992–3 (thousands)

Source: Social Trends 25, Table 7.25

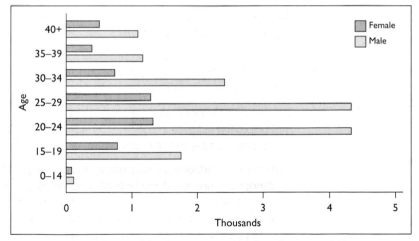

This perspective can also explain the worse morbidity of women. Women are socialised into an unhealthy set of norms and values. They willingly take on responsibilities which make them prone to physical and mental disorder. These include those listed on p. 94, but here the emphasis is on women's choice in doing these things. The social–structural explanation suggests that they are victims of social and economic circumstance.

The stress explanation

Modern medicine now realises that levels of stress can affect people's resistance to disease. Stress may take the form of a constant pressure on the individual from the environment, work, family or social circumstances. Alternatively it may come in short but powerful bursts related to specific life events such as bereavement, divorce and so on. In either case the health effects can be devastating. It is thought that women are particularly subject to stress for the following reasons:

Jessie Bernard and other feminists argue that the isolation and constant decision making involved in housework are very stressful to the women who do it, as is the responsibility of caring for a young child. The effects of this are sometimes referred to as the 'housewife syndrome'.

Women act as the absorbers of stresses for other family members. Functionalists argue that women play the 'affective' (emotional) role in the family and make it into a haven where the 'instrumental' male can recover from the demands of the wider world. Functionalists do not appreciate, though, that acting as counsellor and therapist for the rest of the family takes a toll on the women themselves.

The social situation in which women are placed in most societies means that they carry the burden of stress. In this context, then, stress is related to social structure, so the stress is an adjunct to the social structural–material approach.

Obtain a copy of Cline and Spender's Reflecting Men at Twice Their Natural Size *(1987). Do you agree with their account of the role that women play in inflating men's egos?*

The genetic explanation

Figure 6.7 Caring for women in London: cancer control organised by Lambeth's Health Authority and Borough Council

Women suffer from certain sorts of health problems because of their distinctive biology – that is, there is a range of illnesses which men cannot contract. In particular these are associated with:

pregnancy and childbirth

contraception and abortion

menstruation and menopause

breast and cervical cancer.

In addition there are certain illnesses which women are more likely to suffer from than men because of their different biology:

Because women have a greater immune response than men they suffer far more from auto-immune diseases which occur when the body's defence system attacks a substance which is part of the body itself rather than a foreign object. Arthritis is one of these disorders; it affects women three times more frequently than men.

Because women live longer than men they are more likely to suffer from the 'degenerative diseases' – those associated with ageing.

Men also suffer worse health in some respects and have a higher mortality rate generally because of genetic factors:

Men suffer more heart disease: they lack the hormonal protection that women derive from oestrogens, which are present until the menopause at around 50, at which age women begin to suffer an equal risk of heart disease.

There is some evidence that the chromosome difference between men and women has an effect. Men normally have one X and one Y chromosome; women have two Xs. A study of four generations of an Amish family in Pennsylvania showed that males who were missing the long arm of their Y chromosomes substantially outlived the women. However, in two neighbouring Amish families where the men had normal Y chromosomes (i.e. no deletion), the mortality pattern was normal and the women outlived the men.

What criticisms do you have of the methodology used in this study?

Death rates are greater among males even before social factors have had a chance to come into play – witness the rates for stillbirths, perinatal mortality etc. This shows that genetic rather than social factors are indeed important.

Women and welfare

Laura Balbo (1987) uses the metaphor of a patchwork quilt to discuss women's role in health and welfare. She says that women, through their servicing work in the home and in the NHS, social services and so on, hold modern society (the quilt) together. Society comprises a disorganised and complex array of fragmentary institutions, inadequate resources and poor organisation. Yet it hangs together thanks to the labour of women, which is largely unpaid, usually unrecognised and always undervalued.

> '[Women] patch together resources to meet human needs . . . This packaging of resources requires intelligence, planning, creativity, time and hard work. And just as in a patchwork quilt, the end result is design, logic and order.'

One example of this happening is in the policy of 'care in the community' (see p. 121). Though this is apparently well organised, in practice the burden of care for the sick and the elderly falls predominantly on women. This is neatly summed up in the formula:

community care = family care = care by women.

It is estimated that there are 1.3 million people acting as the principal carers to disabled adults and children. Probably 75 per cent of these are women – the wives, mothers, daughters and daughters-in-law of the disabled. At any one time 20 per cent of women between 40 and 59 years will be providing such care, and probably half of all women will do so at some stage in their lives. Moreover 6.5 million parents act as the primary carer for children under the age of 16 years; in 95 per cent of households the mother is the principal carer.

1 Consider the effects on a woman and on the relationships within the family of caring for a disabled elderly relative in her home. If possible, prepare a structured interview schedule about this issue and conduct one or more interviews with female carers whom you know.

2 Official estimates suggest that informal care by females in the home will be less likely to occur in the future, despite the increasing number of old people in the population and the government's desire to extend community care. Why might this be so?

Professionally, too, women tend to work in the caring professions, especially in the lower levels. The NHS is the single biggest employer of women in this country – 75 per cent of its employees are female. Yet these women are not spread evenly through the hierarchy:

75 per cent of ancillary workers (cleaners, cooks, etc.) are female.

86 per cent of nurses are female.

20 per cent of full-time GPs are female.

Table 6.3 gives some figures for hospital medical staff.

Table 6.3 Hospital medical staff in England, 1985	
Grade	Females as a percentage of total in grade
Consultant and Senior House Medical Officer	23
Associate specialist	12.5
Senior Registrar	23
Registrar	21
Senior House Officer	32
House Officer	39

Source: Adapted from *Health and Personal Social Services Statistics for England 1986*, London: HMSO, 1986

Even where women do reach the higher categories there are male and female specialisms. Consultants in child and adolescent psychiatry and mental handicap are about 10 times more likely to be women than those in surgery of any type. Elsewhere within the NHS, too, there are gender-based specialisms:

- Male nurses are concentrated in psychiatric nursing.

- Female doctors and consultants tend to specialise in obstetrics and paediatrics.

- Almost all of the more than 16,000 midwives in England are female.

Outside the NHS we find that:

- 80 per cent of the staff in old people's homes are women.

- 75 per cent of the staff in children's homes are women.

- Most primary school teachers are women, but few heads are.

- Most social workers in the lower grades are women.

- Women figure prominently in voluntary organisations such as Help the Aged, the Red Cross and so on. Their work is either free or low paid.

Women and medicine

Feminists are critical of the biomedical approach to a number of issues, though fundamentally they all revolve around the point that biomedicine is controlled by men who use their power to the detriment of women's interests. This patriarchal medical practice is most evident in the following areas:

pregnancy and childbirth

contraception.

Pregnancy and childbirth

Hilary Graham and Ann Oakley (1981) have shown that the views held about the nature of childbirth by obstetricians on the one hand and mothers on the other are quite different and lead to conflict. For the obstetrician, childbirth is a medical problem, indistinguishable from other aspects of medical work. Women and their babies are 'cases' and need to be 'dealt with' efficiently (and according to the needs of the hospital – which may mean inducing the baby's birth at a convenient time if necessary). Women, on the other hand, see childbirth as natural, not medical, and as an experience to be savoured rather than got through quickly and safely. Women desire control over the process and over their own bodies, but this is denied by doctors who are in the position to exert control.

Contraception

Feminists note how the technology of contraception has been directed at women far more than men. The only commonly available forms of contraception for the male, the sheath and vasectomy, have very low risks of side effects. Yet every other form, all of which are used by the woman, can have harmful effects. The negative effects of Western (and male-dominated) medicine are confined to women where possible. Contraceptive pills can cause cancer, IUDs and the cap can make women susceptible to infections and other complications. Depo provera (an injectable contraceptive) has been banned in the United States because of its side effects but is still used around the world, including Britain.

Even ancient civilisations gave women a fairly hard time in this area. The ancient Egyptians used crocodile dung pessaries, while camel dung ones were used in the Middle East. The Ancient Greeks and Romans simply killed their unwanted new-born girls. Hebrew women in the time of Christ used sponges dipped in brandy or vinegar.

Essay

'Both present patterns and historical trends in health and illness can only be understood in the context of social and economic systems.' Discuss this statement with particular reference to the different patterns of health and illness among men and women.

Women and social policy

Feminists argue that 'welfare' legislation incorporates the patriarchal ideology of the society that originates it. Legislation such as the Factory Acts of the nineteenth century which were supposedly designed to protect women from working long hours in unsafe conditions were in fact designed to take them out of the workforce and keep them in the home, no longer competing with men for jobs. The 1911 National Insurance Act insured male workers but excluded married women, who were thought to be the responsibility of their husband and dependent on him. The Beveridge Report adopted the same approach: 'the attitude of the housewife to gainful employment outside the home is not and should not be the same as that of the single woman. She has other duties . . .'

Women in part-time jobs today are often denied state benefits because they are not covered by the National Insurance system. Similarly they may find themselves denied non-contributory benefit because, as a result of their child-care responsibilities, they find they are defined as 'not available for work' by the local benefits office. Until the position was altered by a ruling of the European Court in the mid-1980s, men (married or single) and single women could claim benefit for caring for an invalid relative in the home, but married women could not; this was supposed to be part of their normal duties and should therefore not be subsidised by the state.

Even today, then, there is a reluctance to integrate women fully into the Welfare State – or to go very far in replacing the unpaid work of women within the family by welfare institutions. Patrick Jenkin expressed this attitude neatly when he was Secretary of State for the Social Services:

> 'There is now elaborate machinery to ensure that [women have] equal opportunity, equal pay and equal rights but I think we ought to stop and ask, "Where does this leave the family?"'

Examination question

'Women's health chances, the health care they receive and their responsibility for the health care of others – all these can only be understood in the context of their gender roles in a patriarchal society.' Explain and discuss this view.

AEB AS-level, Summer 1994, Paper 2, question 6

A skeleton answer for this question can be found on p. 149.

Bibliography

Arditti, R., Duelli Klein, R. and Minden, S. (1984) *Test Tube Women,* London: Pandora

Baggott, R. (1994) *Health and Health Care in Britain,* New York: St Martin's Press

Balbo, L. (1987) 'Crazy quilts', in Showstack Sassoon (1987), pp. 45–72

Beechey, V. and Whitelegg, E. (eds) (1986) *Women in Britain Today,* Milton Keynes: Open University Press (see especially the chapter by L. Doyal and M. Elston, 'Women, health and medicine')

Bernard, J. (1982) 'The wife's marriage', in M. Evans (ed.) *The Woman Question,* London: Fontana

Cline, S. and Spender, D. (1987) *Reflecting Men at Twice Their Natural Size,* London: Fontana

Cox, B. *et al.* (eds) *The Health and Lifestyle Survey Seven Years On: A Longitudinal Study of a Nationwide Sample, Measuring Changes in Physical and Mental Health, Attitude and Lifestyle,* Aldershot: Dartmouth

Dale, J. and Foster, P. (1986) *Feminists and State Welfare,* London: Routledge

Daly, M. (1979) *Gyn/Ecology,* London:Women's Press

Ehrenreich, B. and English, D. (1973) *Complaints and Disorders: The Sexual Politics of Sickness, London:* Writers and Readers

Finch, J. and Groves, D. (eds) (1983) *A Labour of Love: Women Work and Caring,* London: Routledge

General Household Survey 1993, London: OPCS

Graham, H. (1984) *Women, Health and the Family,* London: Wheatsheaf

—— (1985) *Health and Welfare,* London: Macmillan

—— (1987) 'Women, health and illness', *Social Studies Review,* Vol. 3, No. 1, September, pp. 15–20

—— and Oakley (1981) 'Competing ideologies of reproduction: medical and maternal perspectives on pregnancy', in Roberts (1981)

Miles, A. (1991) *Women, Health and Medicine,* Buckingham: Open University Press

OPCS (1987) *General Household Survey 1985,* London: HMSO

—— (1992) *General Household Survey 1990,* London: HMSO

Pascall, G. (1986) *Social Policy,* London: Tavistock

Roberts, H. (ed.) (1981) *Women, Health and Reproduction,* London: Routledge

—— (1983) *Doing Feminist Research,* London: Routledge

Showstack Sassoon, A. (1987) *From a Woman's Point of View,* London: Hutchinson

UN Human Development Report, New York: Oxford University Press, New York, published annually (useful for international data on mortality and orbidity)

Walker, A. (1982) *Community Care: The Family, the State and Social Policy,* Oxford: Blackwell & Robertson

Useful addresses

Information about countries around the globe, including mortality statistics, is available on the World Wide Web. The CIA World Factbook, for example, contains this sort of data and can be accessed at: http://www.odci.gov/95fact/fb95toc/fb95toc.html (you should replace '95' with the current year).

7 Mental illness

Figure 7.1 Jack Nicholson in the film, *One Flew Over the Cuckoo's Nest.*

This chapter will first examine the nature of mental illness. It will then summarise the evidence about its prevalence in the UK and discuss alternative explanations of these findings.

What is mental illness?

In law mental illness is 'a state of mind which affects the person's thinking, perceiving, emotion or judgement to the extent that she or he requires care or medical treatment in her or his own interests or the interests of other persons'. Less legalistically, we can identify a continuum between mental health and mental illness. We may be at different points on this continuum at different times in our lives (though some may never get nearer to 'mad' than the grey area in the middle occupied by anxiety and depression).

Mental and emotional disorders have been classified as shown in Figure 7.2.

We have already noted that definitions of health and illness are socially constructed.

Figure 7.2

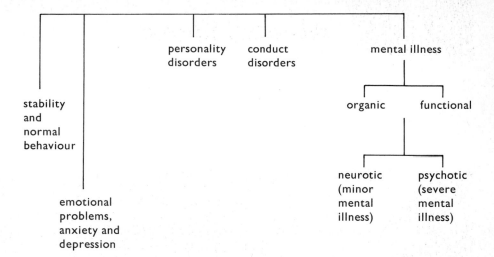

This is just as true for mental health, if not more so. Earlier in British history mental illness was seen as a sign of possession by dark forces, often as retribution for some evil act committed by the ill person. Even into the eighteenth and nineteenth centuries the less educated still explained mental illness in terms of devilish interference, while the more educated explained it in terms of moral weakness and over-indulgence. Gradually during the last century and the early part of this the mentally ill came to be seen as troublesome unfortunates. Today, though, thanks to the medicalisation of mental illness, they are viewed as suffering from a disease analogous to physical disease. The dean of an American university summed this change up when he said about an outbreak of witchcraft practices on campus:

> 'a couple of hundred years ago we would have burned them; twenty-five years ago I would have expelled them. Now we simply send them all to the psychiatrists.'

Today even behaviour traits such as those associated with alcoholism are seen as evidence of disease, whereas in the past some 'fault' would have been ascribed to the person involved.

 Is alcoholism a 'disease', in your view? Grant (1979) provides useful information on this subject.

The statistics

Gender plays an important role in mental health:

Women are twice as likely as men to die from mental disorders (5,189 deaths compared to 2,530 in 1993), though this is linked to their greater longevity. Before the age of 74 men are more likely to die from mental illness, but women are more likely to be admitted to mental hospitals and units.

Informed estimates suggest that women are twice as likely to suffer from some form of mental illness as men are (although boys are more likely to suffer mental illness than adult men). Many of these illnesses will not lead the women to be admitted to a mental hospital, and many will be lost from view in the clinical iceberg.

Twice as many women as men are prescribed psychotropic drugs in a year (20 per cent of women against 10 per cent of men).

Twice as many women as men are admitted to mental hospitals suffering from depressive illness.

Class and ethnic origin are important too:

Black patients are more likely to suffer compulsory admission to mental hospital than whites (though overall immigrants seem to have similar or even lower rates of admission than the indigenous population).

Working-class mothers are more likely to suffer from depression than middle-class mothers.

Recent explanations of mental illness

The organic approach

This is probably the most influential approach in psychiatry. It identifies physical causes as the reasons for mental illness. These may be:

biochemical

physiological (related to the functioning of the whole body)

neurological (to do with the nervous system)

anatomical

endocrinological (concerning the glands that secrete hormones into the blood stream)

genetic.

Psychiatrists have linked certain forms of mental illness to organic causes such as epilepsy, toxins in the body (such as alcohol), nutritional disorders, brain injuries and tumours. For example, dementia is thought to be caused by disturbances in the thyroid gland in the neck which can affect the brain. In 1988 scientists at the Middlesex Hospital identified a genetic defect which they believe may be the cause of schizophrenia, which affects 500,000 people in Britain. Almost all psychiatrists would agree that *some* mental illness is caused by organic disorders; some would even say that *all* mental illness has organic causes.

Clearly, if the aetiology (cause) of the disease is physical, then the cure needs to concentrate on this, not the psychological symptoms. Treatment often involves:

drugs (such as one of the 60 brands of tranquillisers)

electro-convulsive treatment (ECT)

psychosurgery – for example lobotomy, in which the tissue connecting the frontal lobe with other brain centres is severed; modern surgical techniques, however, are more refined than this technique, which was mainly used in the 1950s.

The psychodynamic approach

This approach comes from psychoanalysis, which originated in the work of Sigmund Freud. He believed that we all have very strong drives, particularly the sexual drive (libido), which are not permitted full expression in society. They often give rise to difficulties in relationships, particularly in early life, which leave us with sets of unfulfilled desires, unresolved conflicts, suppressed fears and so on. We are generally not conscious of these, but they can affect our behaviour and in some cases give rise to symptoms of mental illness.

Some exponents of the psychodynamic approach have moved away from Freud's original ideas (some following other figures such as Carl Jung and Wilhelm Reich). However, the underlying principle remains that adult mental illness is the product of early experiences and unconscious, suppressed conflicts which prevent the individual from behaving 'normally'.

Research the work of Jung, Reich or Freud and make a presentation to the group about it. The For Beginners series of handbooks could be a useful starting point.

The psychodynamic treatment of mental illness involves going through a long process of psychotherapy in which the psychiatrist attempts to interpret the patient's conscious ideas and words in order to identify the problem or problems in the past which are the cause of the symptoms. If the patient can be encouraged to recognise the real cause and discuss it with the therapist, the contradictions will be resolved and the symptoms will eventually disappear.

The behaviourist approach

Behaviourists believe that deviant behaviour (including mental illness) is the product of poor training in childhood. Children are taught how to behave through a process called 'conditioning'. Desired behaviour is reinforced through rewards, whereas undesired behaviour is discouraged by punishment or instilling fear (though reward has been found to be more effective than punishment). Thus some sorts of behaviour become associated with pleasure and are repeated, others with pain and are avoided. When this is not done correctly or not done enough the person may behave oddly, or 'exhibit maladaptive responses' in the jargon. Also, if a certain situation or event has been followed by an unpleasant experience in the past, the two things become associated for the patient. Thus seemingly harmless things may give rise to neurotic behaviour; the many phobias are thought to be the product of this sort of accidental conditioning.

The treatment here is to condition the patient into new patterns of behaviour through a process of reinforcing the desired actions and (at least) discouraging the undesired ones. One way of doing this is through aversion therapy – for instance, administering an electric shock in the circumstances which normally lead the patient to perform the undesired behaviour. The aim is that the patient will come to associate that behaviour with the unpleasant shock and so stop doing it. A more positive approach is to encourage 'adaptive responses' by rewarding appropriate behaviour with tokens that can be exchanged for privileges or luxuries.

Figure 7.3 The teacher's dream? Aversion therapy in the classroom!

The systemic approach

According to this approach illness is the product of the circumstances in which the patient lives, in other words the result of a set of personal interactions in a particular context. Systemic theorists have concentrated on the *family* as an important microsystem which can lead to behaviour which is seen as symptomatic of mental illness. The mental hospital itself is another example.

Dr R. D. Laing is the most famous psychiatrist to have subscribed to this school of thought. In a series of case studies of schizophrenia he showed how individuals (often girls and young women) came to exhibit bizarre behaviour as a result of oppressive family relationships (see Laing and Esterson 1974). Often the mother and father treated their daughter in a way which itself could be deemed 'mad': intercepting her letters and listening to telephone calls, discouraging her from seeing boys (yet saying that she should), walking unannounced into her bedroom while she was undressed, treating her like a child (while insisting she should 'grow up') and so on. In such a light the girl's schizophrenic behaviour begins to make sense, but the parents often succeed in labelling their daughter – first as good, then bad, and finally mad. The same point was made by the 'mad' seventeenth century playwright Nathaniel Lee, protesting at being committed to an asylum:

> 'They called me mad, and I called them mad, and damn them, they outvoted me.'

As the child grows up the progression through the good–bad–mad set of labels is a common pattern of election of an individual into the category of the 'mentally ill', and it is usually the family that comes up with the labels.

Erving Goffman's work on mental asylums also shows how a social micro-system works (Goffman 1984). He argues that, far from curing people, asylums (like other 'total institutions' such as prisons) can actually cause personality disorders: 'they are forcing houses for changing persons; each is a natural experiment in what can be done to the self'. In total institutions:

all aspects of life are conducted in same place and under one authority;

all activities are undertaken in the company of a large number of other people, all required to do the same thing together;

all phases of the day's activities are tightly scheduled, the sequence being imposed by formal rules administered by officials;

the enforced activities are supposedly designed to fulfil the official aims of the institution.

What other examples of total institutions can you identify that fulfil these criteria?

The word 'supposedly' is used advisedly in the last point. Goffman argues that the staff in asylums soon begin to suit their own convenience rather than furthering the interests of the patients. Patients are ignored for long periods, given sleeping tablets (so that the staff are not troubled in the night) and encouraged to do the staff's menial jobs 'for the exercise'. Staff themselves are in danger of becoming institutionalised and undergoing personality change. They begin to doubt which side they are on. Their response to this is to become extremely authoritarian to prove they are custodians, not inmates.

What happens to people in total institutions is as follows. First there is a process of 'mortification', which means that the former personality of the new entrant is eradicated and his or her power of self-determination is removed. This may be achieved in any of the following ways:

denial of comforts such as a soft bed and quiet at night

humiliating initiation ceremonies (in some cases)

locking inmates up

restrictions on talking or self-expression (having to call people 'sir', etc.)

removal of personal items such as clothes and jewellery

cutting inmates' hair.

Once the old personality has been rooted out, the entrant to the institution is now ready to be moulded to the pattern of behaviour desired. This is achieved by:

imposing and enforcing 'house rules'

giving rewards and privileges for obedience

punishing those who break the rules.

Do these things occur in the institutions you came up with in the exercise above?

Figure 7.4 Her life would be far worse if she were put in a total institution, according to Goffman.

She's different.
Her life doesn't
have to be.

Without your help we're handicapped.
M E N C A P

Inmates may respond to this pressure by:

withdrawing into an inner world. The inmate refuses to be involved in the world of the total institution. In mental hospitals this is known as 'regression', and may be seen as confirmation that the person is ill rather than as a rational response to the institution itself;

rebelling against the staff. This is very difficult to maintain given their power and again may be taken as a sign of mental illness;

becoming institutionalised – seeing the total institution as a safe and desirable place to be and the outside world as threatening;

conversion – becoming over-compliant, using the terminology of the staff, never disagreeing with them, being obsequious.

Do these behaviours also occur in your examples?

Behaviour associated with any of these responses would, in the outside world, be considered 'mad' or at least odd. A number of additional factors mean that the released inmate finds reintegration into wider society difficult. These include disculturation (loss or failure to acquire the habits currently required), the stigma attached to being a former inmate, the problem of once again being a small fish in a big pond rather than the reverse, and finally the fact that even on the outside there may still be some restrictions on behaviour.

The social approach

This approach stresses broader social factors than the systemic approach to mental illness. While the latter is microscopic in orientation (and is associated with the interactionist school in sociology – see p. 22), the social approach is macroscopic. The systemic approach looks at labelling and the medical process, particularly in total institutions. It also blames the family; according to the social approach we need to look further afield to find the causes of mental illness. Such factors as the following are thought to be to blame:

poverty

social isolation caused by living in blocks of flats and depressing environments

mundane, repetitive work

overcrowding

stressful life events, such as divorce, exams, births and deaths

sexual inequality and limiting gender roles

consumerism

unemployment

instrumental relationships based on rigid hierarchies

the stresses and strains that all this engenders.

This approach helps to explain the social class and gender inequalities in mental as well as physical health. It moves the study and recommendations for the treatment of mental illness into the realm of sociology, complementing the work done by psychologists and psychiatrists. It regards as completely misconceived the systemic approach to the mentally ill, which it interprets as saying: 'Our attempts to cure the mentally ill have only resulted in harm – let's allow the community to try to help them.' The result is 'decarceration' – ejecting the mentally ill from the total institutions criticised by Goffman and others, only to throw them back into the social context that caused their illness in the first place. Similarly blaming the family, as Laing does in some of his work, fails to recognise the initial causes of the family's 'mad' behaviour.

The answer, according to those who subscribe to this perspective, lies in group therapy and the establishment of therapeutic communities. We should try to set up cohesive groups for people with problems. They should give each other mutual support and a degree of protection from the problems listed above.

The view that mental illness is a myth

Some psychiatrists think that most mental illness is not really illness at all in the medical sense. Thomas Szasz (1973), for example, believes that mental illness does not exist. Labels such as agoraphobia, hysteria, obsessive-compulsive neurosis, depression, paranoia and so on are attached to people as if they were things that happened to them (like catching a cold). This is nothing more than a convenient means to deal with socially disruptive problems. What medicine is saying in such cases is (for example), 'People shouldn't be afraid of open spaces, therefore agoraphobics are ill and need treatment to normalise them.' Szasz counters:

> 'I hold that mental illness is a metaphorical disease; that, in other words, bodily illness stands in the same relation to mental illness as a defective television receiver stands to an objectionable television programme.'

According to this view, there is really no difference between contemporary Western treatment of the mentally ill and the old Soviet practice of locking dissidents up in mental hospitals. In both cases the assumption is that only mad people question the social and economic system. This is nothing more than social control under another name.

Having read the various explanations of the causes of mental illness, and when you have done some further reading (see the bibliography at the end of this chapter), complete the following table:

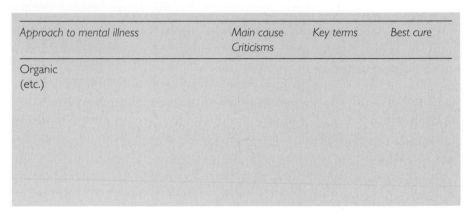

Approach to mental illness	Main cause Criticisms	Key terms	Best cure
Organic (etc.)			

A patient, Mrs A, is referred to a psychiatrist because she has a compulsion to wash her hands constantly. She says that the air and physical surfaces are polluted with germs and she is terrified of becoming ill through contact with them. She even constantly blows away the air in front of her mouth. She shows classic symptoms of an obsessional neurosis. How would each of the above perspectives interpret these symptoms and how would they treat this illness?

Essay

How far are sociological explanations of mental illness different from and critical of medical ones?

Bibliography

Asen, E. (1986) *Psychiatry for Beginners,* London: Writers and Readers

Busfield, J. (1989) *Managing Madness,* London: Hutchinson

Croyden Smith, A. (1982) *Schizophrenia and Madness,* London: Unwin Hyman

Gibbs, A . (1986) *Understanding Mental Health,* London: Consumers Association/Hodder

Goffman, E. (1984) *Asylums,* Harmondsworth: Penguin (first published 1961)

Grant, M. (1979) *Alcoholism in Perspective,* London: Croom Helm

Laing, R. D. and Esterson, A. (1974) *Sanity, Madness and the Family,* Harmondsworth: Penguin (first published 1964)

Porter, R. A. (1987) *Social History of Madness: Stories of the Insane,* London: Weidenfield & Nicholson

Rycroft, C. (1971) *Reich,* London: Fontana

Sedgwick, P. (1982) *Psycho-Politics,* London: Pluto

Szasz, T. (1973) *The Myth of Mental Illness,* St Albans: Paladin (first published 1962)

Wollheim, R. (1971) *Freud,* London: Fontana

Also helpful are the For Beginners books, published by Writers and Readers. These deal with many of the founders of psychiatry.

8 Debates on the Welfare State

HAPPY CHRISTMAS FROM THE HOMELESS

YOUR £10 WILL HELP CRISIS GIVE HOMELESS PEOPLE A HOME THIS CHRISTMAS.   CALL 0500 10 99 99 NOW.

Figure 8.1

This chapter is designed to introduce you to some of the important debates in the field of health, welfare and poverty. It can be used as a stimulus for:

- formal debates

- further research (both local and national)

- simulations

- brainstorming.

The areas covered are:

- biomedicine versus alternative medicine

- the social 'problem' of ageing

- 'community care' for the mentally handicapped and others

- the debate about underfunding of the health service

- the role of the professions

- the effect of the Welfare State on social inequality
- public versus private medicine
- drugs in society.

Biomedicine versus alternative (or 'complementary') therapies

Biomedicine is the approach to medicine that is dominant in most countries in the world today. It has the following characteristics:

It is 'scientific' – that is, it deals only with observable phenomena, uses the experimental method, and seeks to establish laws to build up a body of knowledge.

It sees the body as physical machine, the parts of which need to be 'fixed' or even replaced when they 'go wrong'.

Chemical (drugs), physical (surgery) and even electrical (ECT) and radiation treatments are the most successful.

Biomedicine sees the world as threatening and its role as responding to 'invasions' by viruses, bacteria, rickettsias, fungi, protozoans and the rest ('germs' in common parlance). This 'allopathic' approach – using treatments that produce effects opposite to those of the ailment – seeks to defend the body from attack by the aggressive use of 'magic bullets' of one sort or another, such as chemicals, radiation, etc. In some cases this involves the actual use of guns.

This approach is summed up in the following statement from G. Barry *et al.* (1965):

> 'At birth you were as free of germs as the carefully sterilized instruments of the doctor who delivered you. But from the moment you took your first breath, germs entered your nose and throat; when you were first put into your cradle, germs came into contact with your skin, and from the moment you swallowed your first food, germs invaded your digestive system.'

The critique of biomedicine is based on the following points:

Some writers have noticed a similarity to religious thinking – the idea that sick people have been invaded by evil spirits. The allopathic approach takes the wrong attitude to both the body and the environment. It does not ask why we can usually tolerate 'germs' without becoming ill, or why we do sometimes become susceptible to them. The 'holistic' approach of, for example, homeopathy (see below) does address these sorts of questions (holism means they do not treat the disease, rather they treat the patient, taking into account all aspects of his or her life, environment, personal relationships and so on).

Biomedicine is based on a division between mind and body – seeing the two as opposed rather than forming a whole. This is referred to as 'Cartesian dualism' (from the work of the French philosopher René Descartes). In biomedicine Cartesian dualism results in the following sorts of oppositions:

Mind   versus   Body

Spirit   versus   Matter

Person   versus   Disease (medical cases)

A holistic approach rejects this dualism and sees mind and body as inseparable, a whole. One cannot be understood without an appreciation of the other.

Biomedicine works for the current social system rather than for the ill person. For example it treats the symptoms of disease (headache, deviant behaviour associated with mental illness) rather than the conditions that caused them (poor environments, hazardous and stressful work).

Biomedicine claims to have a monopoly over effective treatment; other approaches are condemned as quackery. It uses the ideology of science to back up these claims and marshals the legislators to enforce them. (Legislation in 1858 set up the medical register and prevented doctors on it from cooperating with unqualified practitioners.)

Biomedicine directs the resources of the nation into the wrong areas – for example, mechanical intervention such as spare part surgery and heart operations instead of health education and preventative medicine. This is partly because doctors want to keep medical knowledge to themselves, partly because of the biomechanical approach which treats the body as a machine. The NHS, under the influence of biomedicine, is not a national health service but a national *sickness* service – a fire brigade for illness rather than a defender of good health.

Biomedicine does more harm than good. Doctor-caused illness ('iatrogenesis') accounts for much of the ill-health in Britain and other industrialised countries. Two fifths of patients taking prescribed drugs suffer some side-effects. Many of the investigative procedures of biomedicine are themselves painful and damaging. Many conditions, such as migraine and back pain, are not effectively tackled by biomedical approaches, and attempts to do so cause problems in themselves.

In reply, the proponents of biomedicine argue that there is no firm evidence of the success of other approaches, but their own profession has been highly successful in curing many diseases, ridding the developed world of others and generally alleviating suffering.

Research the evidence to back up these claims. Sources that may be helpful are Social Trends *for Britain and, for abroad, some of the reference texts in the bibliography for Chapter 3.*

Furthermore biomedicine does now recognise the importance of psychological factors in health. Biomedics are no longer Cartesian dualists.

The alternatives to biomedicine

A study conducted by MORI in 1989 for *The Times* found that 27 per cent of respondents had used complementary medicines and that 87 per cent would 'seriously consider' doing so. There are as many as 135 different types of therapy that are alternatives or complementary to the biomedical approach. They range from the physical (such as osteopathy and the Alexander technique) through the psychological

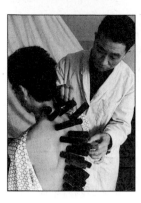

Figure 8.2 Alternative medicine from China

(such as hypnotherapy) to the paranormal (such as faith healing). Below is a list of some of the better-known examples:

homeopathy

osteopathy

chiropractic

herbalism

acupuncture and the Chinese medical system

naturopathy

phytotherapy

iridology

aromatherapy

hydrotherapy.

They have the following points in common:

They place more emphasis than biomedicine on preventing illness rather than curing it.

They are holistic, recognising the importance of mind, body and environment. While they recognise the existence of 'germs', they stress that the person has to be susceptible for illness to result. A professor of hygiene at Munich University drank a solution of pure cholera organisms for a bet in 1892 and nothing happened. Over 40 scientists replicated the experiment, and nothing happened to any of them either!

Their treatments tend to be less toxic and invasive than those of biomedicine.

Generally, unlike biomedicine, they do not claim to be universally effective or to have the answer to all diseases.

A survey by *Which?* magazine found that two thirds of Consumers' Association members who used alternative or complementary therapies did so after experiencing ineffective or painful biomedical intervention. The vast majority were happy with their experience, most having tried homeopathy, osteopathy or herbalism.

Homeopathy is perhaps the most accepted of the complementary therapies (the Queen has a homeopathic doctor). It holds that the symptoms presented by the sick person are not caused by the disease but by the body's action in fighting it off. Anything that can reinforce this will help the body. Therefore substances are given which, in a healthy person, produce the symptoms that occur when the disease is present. These are identified by a process called 'proving' – testing them on healthy people and noting the body's response. Dosages given to ill patients are tiny: the substances are heavily diluted. There is some evidence that homeopathy is effective. Studies in the mid-1970s showed that it was effective in treating rheumatoid arthritis. The death rate during a cholera epidemic in the mid-nineteenth century was found to be much lower in a homeopathic hospital than in a biomedical one.

Acupuncture

This practice, developed in ancient China, is based on the theory that there is a connection between body organs and body surface. Acupuncture involves using needles to stimulate acupuncture points under the skin in an attempt to influence the related organs. It is also claimed that acupuncture has a more general effect in promoting relaxation and relieving pain.

Homeopathy

A system of medicine based on the principle that agents which produce certain signs and symptoms in healthy people cure the same signs and symptoms of disease. The more a particular drug is diluted, the more potent it will be as a cure. Furthermore, the treatment given will be tailored to the individual, rather than to the characteristics of the disease as is generally the case in mainstream biomedicine.

Chiropractic

This is a manipulative therapy designed to maintain the spinal column in a good state of health, without the use of drugs. The therapy is aimed at dealing with specific disorders such as back and neck pain, and headaches.

Herbal medicine

The use of plants and herbs to deal with specific illnesses and to maintain health. A related therapy – aromatherapy – involves body massage using oils extracted from plants.

Hypnotherapy

The inducement of trance has been used to combat a variety of psychological disorders such as anxiety, phobias and insomnia. Hypnotherapy is sometimes used by individuals who are trying to change unhealthy lifestyles such as smoking. Hypnotherapy has also been used in the treatment of conditions with physical symptoms where there may be an underlying psychological cause.

Each member of your group should research one of the complementary therapies. Make a presentation on it to the group as a whole. You might find this structure useful for your presentation:

Explanation
Background
Nature of the treatment
Comparison/contrast with biomedicine
Does it work?
If so, how does it work?

The bibliography for this chapter contains some suggested reading for research and the addresses of some of the centres for these techniques in Britain.

Scientific versus holistic medicine: the arguments

Document A

Here's Health magazine declares it 'is committed to alternative or holistic medicine which treats people rather than disease' and that 'it recognises that given the chance the body will heal itself'.

But just how realistic is that claim? . . . It is nonsense to say conventional medicine is not holistic. Alternative practitioners relate holism to some undiscovered 'natural life force', whereas in scientific medicine holism is based on well-defined neuroendocrine pathways that link mind and body. These sensitive servo-mechanisms give us an enormous capacity for self-healing.

But what about the efficacy of alternative therapies? One recent trial of healing hypertension by laying on of hands provided intriguing evidence. Patients treated by a healer, sometimes at a distance without the patient's knowledge, showed a significant reduction in blood pressure. It sounds convincing. However, the trial also included a control group who received no treatment at all but who thought they might. They too showed a satisfactory reduction.

This study illustrates the power of the placebo effect, often adduced as evidence favouring alternative medicine. The demarcation between scientific and alternative medicine is thus a question of quality of evidence, not the treatment itself . . . I recently examined one young woman who almost certainly had early breast cancer, with a 95 per cent chance of cure by limited surgery. Sadly, she was persuaded to take 'holistic' treatments. If, by remote chance, it is not cancer, alternative practitioners will claim success; but if it is, and progresses, she can be blamed for not following her treatment strictly. This applies to many people with cancer. Modern medicine is their best hope.

Source: Professor M. Baum, 'Considering the alternatives', *Observer*, 19 June 1988

Document B

Orthodox medicine has little time for the fringe – and vice versa. The orthodox fear the very real dangers associated with an upsurge of quacks and charlatans taking people's money and promising them the earth. The fringe fear that modern orthodox medicine is too bigoted and blinkered to be able to recognise a useful fringe therapy if it saw it . . . I make no apologies for the fact that I approach patients as people who are highly complex physical and spiritual creatures. Modern medical 'plumbing' has no attraction for me and I know from experience that I am not alone! The very nature of a medical care system that treats all patients with the same disease label as though they were the same person militates against the individual treatment that people so enjoy and look for in their medical care . . . A person isn't a motor-car – and is more than a collection of parts. In fact the more people know about the parts, the more questions they find. The notion, cherished by the popular press, that modern medicine is now nearer to understanding what humans are all about is completely false. Western and other therapists have huge and fundamental differences of opinion about the basic nature of the body. To many natural therapists the body's energy patterns are supremely important, yet orthodox physicians don't even admit that they exist. The functions of organs such as the liver are differently interpreted by many different therapists and so on. We know a little about the plumbing, but by no means all there is to know.

Source: Dr Andrew Stanway, Alternative Medicine (1986)

1 *Why is modern, scientific, medicine unwilling to recognise the existence of 'life forces' or 'energy patterns'?*

2 *What differences in the interpretation of the word 'holism' may there be between Professor Baum and Dr Stanway?*

3 *Dr Stanway's piece gives a clue as to why alternative medicines are not keen on controlled experiments in which groups of patients with the same disease are treated alternatively and compared with a control group who are not. What is the source of this reluctance?*

4 *What are your views on this debate. How would you back them up?*

The 'problem' of ageing

There were over 9 million old age pensioners in the UK in 1988. By 2040 about one fifth of the population of Britain will be over 60 years old.

Figure 8.3 The increase in the elderly population of the UK (% of total population over 65 years old)

Source: Baggott (1994), Figure 1.3

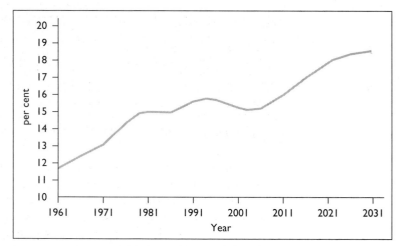

Before reading this section, brainstorm in a group the reasons why the elderly are increasing as a proportion of the British population.

Sociologists and policy makers tend to think of an increasingly ageing population in terms of the 'problems' they present.

The problem approach

The old are a burden to the rest of society. They increase the dependency ratio (i.e. the proportion of those who are not economically active – primarily the young and the old – compared to those who are). In 1993/4 almost half of social security spending (£36.8 billion out of a total of £80.9 billion) went on old age pensioners. The costs of all this are going to escalate, increasing the tax burden of those in work and diverting resources from investment which could improve the economy and general wealth of the country, as Table 8.1 illustrates.

1 *Summarise the trends revealed by Table 8.1.*

2 *If you were in a position to advise the government on alternative responses to these trends, what would be your advice?*

Figure 8.4 Britain in the
twenty-first century?

Table 8.1 Demographic factors affecting pensions

Year	Pensioners (millions)	National Insurance contributors (millions)	Ratio of NI contributors to pensioners
1985	9.3	21.8	2.3
1995	9.8	21.9	2.2
2005	10.0	22.2	2.2
2015	11.1	22.4	2.0
2025	12.3	21.9	1.8
2035	13.2	21.8	1.6

Source: DHSS (1985)

Old age generally brings degenerative diseases, decline in hearing and sight, loss of
memory and IQ (with scores down to the level of a 10 year old by the early 60s
in many cases). The incidence of long-term sickness and days of restricted activity
increases sharply in old age. Over half those over 65 suffer the former, and elderly
women especially suffer from the latter (48 days a year for women between 65
and 74 compared to 34 for men in the same age range).

The decline in the birth rate plus the increase in geographical mobility mean that
many old people are alone. About 25 per cent have no children to help them.
Usually the male of an elderly couple dies first, leaving the female to cope (there
are twice as many women as men over 80 years old).

About 17 per cent of people over 75 need (and get) some form of regular care
(either in residential institutions or in the community).

The Family Expenditure Survey has recorded the resources of households for over 30
years. The trend over this time has been that their resources are declining relative to
those of the non-elderly. They are increasingly likely to be found among the poorest
of society. Nearly two thirds of the elderly (about 5 million people) live in or near
the margins of poverty, according to Peter Townsend (quoted in Graham 1985).

Recently, however, the partial nature of this 'problem' approach has come to be
recognised and the benefits of long-life are now given more emphasis.

The benefits approach

More old age pensioners have income additional to the state pension than ever before, and more have capital assets (especially houses). More than 40 per cent of the over 60s own their home outright, half of the married couples of this age have their own car and half of the over 65s take a package holiday abroad each year.

Better health care means that many medical problems can be eased or even cured.

The greater spending power of the elderly means that the commercial sector is catering for them to a much greater extent than in the past: this is true of the mass media, holiday companies, financial services and so on. The elderly now have great opportunities for leisure, the development of new interests and giving more attention to old ones.

Illustrate this point with examples.

The General Household Survey shows that 75 per cent of the over 65s are in good health. Only 3 per cent live in communal homes or hospitals, and only 20 per cent suffer from senile dementia. Because of improvements in the health of elderly people death rates have declined dramatically. The mortality rate for those aged between 65 and 74 has been declining steadily since 1946, especially to the benefit of men.

While on average there is a decline in faculties as one ages, this is by no means an even process. Third Age Research found that there were many sprightly 80 year olds as well as frail and senile people in their 60s. A physically and mentally active life in adulthood can increase one's 'durability'.

Though the elderly may make greater use of health and social services than other sections of the population, they have also made a greater contribution by paying taxes and National Insurance contributions during their lives. They are receiving what is rightfully theirs, not charity.

The many active elderly people have a lot to contribute to society and wish to make that contribution. However, the attitudes about the elderly that are prevalent (they are dependent, have probably lost their marbles, etc.) make it difficult for them to be accepted.

Brainstorm the following question:
In what fields could the elderly make the greatest contribution to society?

We may now be witnessing the development of a new set of social norms in which old age is viewed positively (as it is in many non-industrial countries as well as some industrialised ones). The American Association of Retired Persons (AARP) has 29 million members and uses the slogans 'Glad to be Gray' and 'Gray Power'. Gray Power is working there: such a large voting block means that they can successfully put proposals for legislation to Congress. The Gumpies (Grown-up Mature Persons) are fighting back. A British ARP has recently been set up with similar goals.

The truth of the matter is that there are two nations in retirement: the poor and the reasonably well off. Which category a particular person falls into largely depends upon their employment patterns during their working career.

Figure 8.5 Pensioners standing up for their rights in London

What are the employment characteristics most likely to determine which group an individual joins in retirement? Which sections of the population are most likely to have those characteristics?

The debate about 'community care' (or 'decarceration')

'Community care' refers to the policy of looking after the elderly, the mentally ill and handicapped in *society* rather than in hospitals and other institutions. It has been vigorously pursued by successive governments. The number of people living permanently in hospitals or residential homes shrank by 63,000 between 1971 and 1981 (Census figures). During the 1980s around half of the long-term institutions in the UK were closed. Norman Fowler, then Secretary of State for Social Services, told the House of Commons in 1986 that:

> 'we shall continue to move towards community care for the mentally handicapped and other groups of patients'.

He cited the cases of South East Thames Regional Health Authority, which by March 1987 would no longer have any children in mental handicap hospitals, and Oxford, where the 'outdated' Bradwell Grove hospital would be closed, 'allowing the staff to be deployed to care for people in community units'. Despite the government's apparent pride in this policy it has been the subject of great debate.

'Community care' is thought to be desirable for several reasons:

The community can act as a support for the mentally ill – social relationships have been found to be beneficial in most cases.

The development of long-acting, injectable drugs means that symptoms can be controlled by monthly treatments during a visit, rather than daily oral intake.

Community care is cheaper than hospital care. It costs £560 per week to look after a mentally ill person in hospital, compared to £7 per week for those in the community (*Guardian*, 26 September 1995).

The range of welfare provision and the number of welfare agencies now available in the community means that it is no longer necessary to shut people away.

Asylums have been shown by Goffman and others to be detrimental to the mental health of patients (see p. 106).

Local health and social services departments are responsible for the aftercare of psychiatric patients leaving hospital (under the 1983 Mental Health Act). Under the 1991 Care Programme approach individual care plans are prepared for people using specialist mental health services. These involve a keyworker who co-ordinates and reviews the plan. Within the social services the approach called Care Management is used. Introduced in 1993, this is similar to the Care Programme approach and involves the use of care managers who assess individuals' needs.

Community care sounds like the perfect solution; even the name has a cosy ring to it. It is a rather ambiguous term, though. It is unclear whether it means care *in* the community (by professionals) or care *by* the community. In the 1960s the first interpretation was the dominant one; today the latter is preferred. Of course, the concept assumes that there is a 'community' to move into. The term 'decarceration' is preferred by Andrew Scull (1984). This is the opposite of incarceration (which means putting people into prison-like institutions) and stresses ejection from institutions rather than care in the community.

The are several problems with the policy of decarceration:

Patients are simply thrown into the most run-down areas of cities and seaside resorts where there is little or no community.

Patients are given little in the way of aftercare facilities such as the provision of employment, specialised accommodation and social support, despite the obligation placed on local authorities to provide them by the 1983 Mental Health Act. They are simply dumped. So there is neither 'community' nor 'care'.

Unscrupulous landlords specialise in providing rooms for ex-inmates. They have no medical training and little or no knowledge of patients' histories. This often results in scandalous overcrowding, poor facilities, sometimes violence and rapid expulsion for being too troublesome. Rents, paid by the authorities, are nonetheless very high.

Private residential care homes for the elderly are relatively unregulated, and there have been several cases of maltreatment within them.

Many of those decarcerated are old as well as mentally ill and have special problems and needs, which makes the lack of care particularly painful for them.

Figure 8.6 Going to church:
Christmas morning at St
Lawrence's hospital for the
mentally handicapped,
Surrey

The most disturbed patients are precisely the ones who will not realise that they
need help and so they will simply drift into oblivion until a serious problem occurs,
bringing them to the attention of the police or medical services.

There have been several recent cases of killings by mentally disturbed patients who
had been released into the community care. In 1992 Christopher Clunis stabbed

Figure 8.7 Places in
residential homes, by
sector

Source: Baggott (1994),
Figure 10.1, p. 223

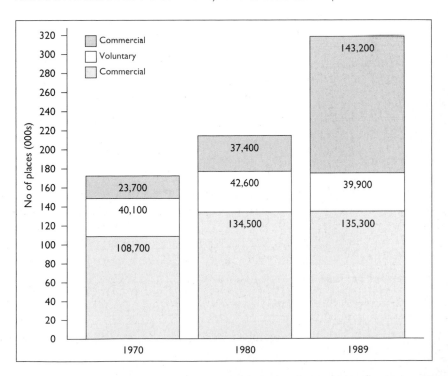

Jonathan Zito to death in a London underground station; Clunis had a history of schizophrenia. Jason Mitchell, a 24-year-old schizophrenic, killed his father and an elderly couple in December 1994 after being released from a secure psychiatric hospital. In 1995 Bryan Bennett was killed in East London by a fellow day care patient with a history of violence and mental illness. The 1995 Mental Health (Patients in the Community) Act gave new powers of 'supervised discharge' which enabled professionals to ensure, in consultation with patients, that they live at known addresses, take medication and so on. This Act has been generally welcomed by relevant professions.

Despite these problems, most psychiatrists and social workers agree that treatment in the community is the best solution for many of the groups this policy affects. They maintain, though, that there are currently insufficient resources devoted to seeing it through, and this is the main reason for many of the current problems. Many of those involved see the closure of hospitals in the 1980s as essentially a cost-cutting exercise. Most of the £2,000 million saved has not been reallocated to agencies responsible for care in the community. The Mental Health Foundation, in a report published in 1994, suggests that at least another £450 million will need to be spent on community care if it is to be done properly. One of the key areas that needs improvement and resources is the communication between the different agencies involved in community care, particularly health, social and criminal justice agencies. This was revealed after an inquiry into the Clunis case showed that these institutions were not sharing information.

> *Read (some of) Erving Goffman's Asylums and (some of) Scull's Decarceration (or the extract from it in Trowler 1987). Formulate the policy you would want implemented if you were Minister of Health.*

Figure 8.8 Spending on the mentally ill

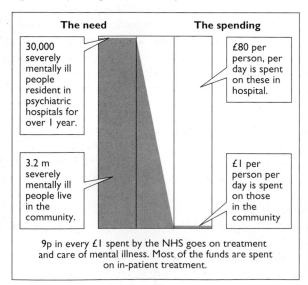

9p in every £1 spent by the NHS goes on treatment and care of mental illness. Most of the funds are spent on in-patient treatment.

Source: Guardian Education, 26 September 1995

Figure 8.9 Psychiatric hospital patients

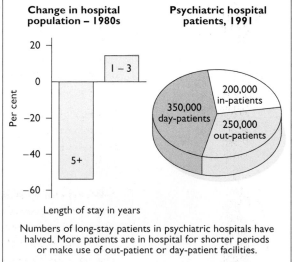

Numbers of long-stay patients in psychiatric hospitals have halved. More patients are in hospital for shorter periods or make use of out-patient or day-patient facilities.

Source: Guardian Education, 26 September 1995

Figure 8.10

Examination question

Critically assess differing sociological perspectives on the role of the family and community in the provision of welfare.

AEB A-level, Winter 1994, Paper 2, question 6

Examine the map on p. 126. The mental hospital (built in the middle of the last century) opposite the council estate in Factory Road has been gradually losing its patients as a result of a policy of community care and of more successful treatment and control of patients through drugs. The hospital is due to close in two years' time. Meanwhile the local social services department plans to buy two empty houses in Willowtree Drive to set up a community hostel for a small number of patients currently in the hospital. This plan has been leaked to the press and residents in the area have called for a public meeting to discuss the issue and to allow them to air their views. Choose roles from those outlined below and spend about 15 minutes planning your arguments for the public meeting. Then hold the meeting.

Director of Social Services and staff (including Finance Director)

You should be prepared to put forward the advantages of the policy of community care in general and the points in favour of a hostel in this location in particular. You are very keen to see the hospital closed for a variety of reasons.

Residents around Willowtree Drive

You are concerned about a number of issues. You are prepared to admit some of your worries (danger to children from the residents of the hostel, etc.) but are rather embarrassed about others (such as falling property prices). You do not wish to be seen to be against the interests of the mental patients and so you want to be able to make an alternative proposal rather than simply block this one.

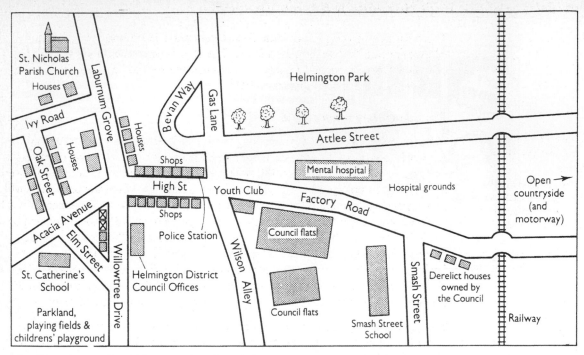

⊠ = Empty houses planned for use as hostel

Figure 8.11 Helmington

Council tenants

You should consider your views about the closure of the mental hospital near to your estate and give careful thought to any alternative plans that the Social Services Department might have should they meet stiff opposition to the Willowtree Drive proposal.

The press

You should take notes on the meeting and, after it has finished, find a quiet room to rough out a headline and a brief summary of the article you would write about it for the local paper (the Helmington Gazette).

The Vicar of Helmington

You should form your own view on this issue, but bear in mind the feelings of your parishioners.

The chair of the meeting

Your role is to be impartial and to make sure that there is an orderly debate in which all sides are heard.

Councillors

Helmington District Council is a 'hung' council, i.e. no one political party holds overall control. Helmshire County Council, though, is Conservative controlled. Represented are district councillors from the Liberal Democrats, Conservatives and Labour, and county councillors from the Conservatives. These should formulate their parties' views on the issue (and their own, if these differ).

Senior administrators from the hospital

You are worried about your jobs and any changes to them once the hospital closes. You are concerned to defend the work of the mental hospital and to save it from closure if you can.

The debate about underfunding of the health service

There has been an ongoing political debate during the 1980s and 1990s about whether or not the NHS is underfunded. The government maintains that there has been an increase in spending since 1979 and that the service continues to improve. Here we examine the arguments on both sides.

The adequately funded NHS

Figure 8.12 The real cost of the National Health Service

£ billion, adjusted to 1993–4 prices using the GDP market prices deflator; planned expenditure for 1994–5

Source: Social Trends 25, Figure 8.14

Although public expenditure grew during the 1980s, it reduced as a proportion of national income from 43 per cent in 1979 to 38 per cent in 1990 (though there was a slight increase between then and 1993). This was in line with government policy, driven by New Right ideology, of reducing the role of the state. However, the proportion of public spending devoted to the NHS rose from its norm of around 10 per cent of total public expenditure in the 1950s and 1960s to 11 per cent in 1981 and 14 per cent by 1990. The NHS has therefore fared well in a general context of reduction in public expenditure as a proportion of total spending. Spending on housing, by contrast, fell from 3 per cent to 1.9 per cent of total public spending during the same period. This relatively fortunate position is reflected in the fact that NHS spending increased by 20 per cent in real terms (i.e. after allowing for inflation) between 1980 and 1989.

International comparisons demonstrate that at 5.3 per cent of national income the level of UK spending on health care is around the average for all OECD countries (5.6 per cent). Where there is a big difference is in spending by the population on private health care. If there needs to be an increase in spending on health anywhere, it is here. We should therefore welcome recent government proposals to give tax relief on health insurance contributions.

The continued growth in the NHS budget can be attributed to several factors:

There is continued and increasing demand for NHS services as medical technology improves and more treatments become available, and as an ageing population places more demands on it.

Media interest in the NHS has given difficulties for ministers who wished to hold back on expenditure in this area.

Figure 8.13 The entrance to the Chelsea and Westminster Hospital opened in 1984

Parliament too often acts in defence of the NHS as there is wide cross-party support for maintaining expenditure on the service. When she was Minister of Health Virginia Bottomley had a very difficult time in the media and in Parliament when she announced the closure of some London hospitals, for example. She soon found herself in a less prestigious government post.

Pressure groups such as the British Medical Association and the Royal Colleges as well as a range of patient groups operate very effectively in defence of the NHS.

Underfunding in the NHS

The growth in spending on the NHS is much less significant than it seems. The costs of health services have risen much more sharply than general prices, and when this is taken into account the growth in NHS expenditure was only around 1.8 per cent per year between 1979 and 1990 (Robinson 1990). Also, different parts of the service fared rather differently. While resources devoted to the hospitals and community sector grew by only 0.9 per cent during the 1980s, the family practitioner services grew by 3.1 per cent.

This analysis of underfunding is supported by the House of Commons Social Services Committee. It suggested in 1988 that the NHS was underfunded by around £1.9 billion and proposed a two-year rescue plan, with £1 billion spent in each year on the NHS. More recently the National Association of Health Authorities put the shortfall that had accumulated between 1980 and 1990 at £4.4 billion.

Even according to the Department of Health's own estimates a growth rate of 1.8 per cent per year is lower than is required to maintain and improve the service in a context of demographic change, developments in medical technology, new disease patterns and so on. The Department suggests that an annual growth rate of 2 per cent is necessary to keep pace with these changes.

International comparisons also support the 'underfunding' case, as Figure 8.14 shows.

 Welfare spending in 1993 accounted for about two thirds of all UK government spending and over a quarter of the total output of the country (Gross Domestic Product or GDP). The total cost of spending on health, social security, social services, housing and education in 1993 was £160 billion. What arguments are there in support of and against maintaining or even increasing this level of expenditure? If you are working in a large group, divide into two sub-groups to examine each side of this question.

The debate about the role of the professions

W. J. Goode (1978) cites two core characteristics of a profession:

- prolonged specialised training in a body of abstract thought

- a collectivity or service orientation (i.e. working for other people).

Associated with these are ten further characteristics:

The profession determines its own standards of education and training.

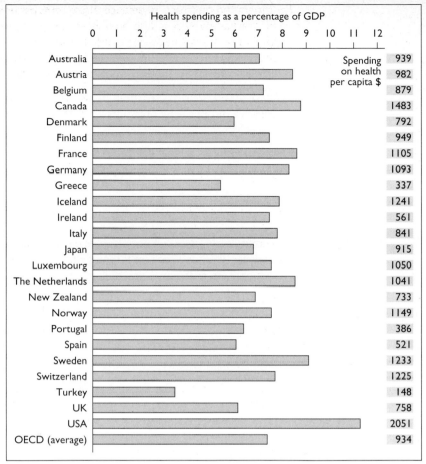

Figure 8.14 Cross-national comparisons of health expenditure, OECD countries, 1987

Source: Baggott (1994), Figure 7.1

The student goes through a deeper socialisation experience than learners in other occupations.

Professional practice is recognised by some form of licence.

Licensing and admission boards are staffed by members of the profession.

Most legislation concerned with the profession is shaped by it.

There are high rewards in terms of income, power and prestige so that high-calibre students can be attracted.

The practitioner is relatively free of evaluation and control by lay people.

The norms of practice enforced by the profession are more stringent than legal controls.

Members are more strongly identified and affiliated with the profession than is usual in other occupations.

Members do not normally leave the profession and are usually happy to be in it.

According to these criteria, would you regard the following as professionals? If not, why not?

nurses, teachers, solicitors, prostitutes ('the oldest profession'), chiropodists, senior policemen/women, soldiers, social workers.

For functionalist sociologists the higher professions such as medicine are virtually beyond reproach. Professionals are seen as selfless individuals working for the good of the community, often making great personal sacrifices. They need to be of the highest intelligence and skill, have to undergo years of training and in their early careers earn very little. High levels of reward later, then, are necessary to attract, retain and motivate the best people into the professions.

Against this altruistic view of the professionals, however, the following charges have been levelled:

There is very little control over them. Professional bodies (such as the General Medical Council) are charged with supervising the profession. But, being members of that profession, they usually whitewash or ignore cases of incompetence, etc. Final sanctions, like striking a doctor off the medical register, are used only rarely and then more often for sexual misconduct than for gross incompetence.

Professionals use the argument of 'professional expertise' as a smokescreen for practices which in other areas would not be permitted, for example maintaining a monopoly over the provision of particular goods or services, price fixing and so on. Examples are numerous; the restriction on advertising the services of solicitors and opticians was only recently lifted. The professionals claimed that the prohibition maintained the level of the service by preventing over-concentration on price. Actually it was to maintain profits by preventing 'harmful' competition between members of the same profession.

They artificially restrict numbers entering the profession in order to increase demand for those already in it and therefore raise the fees they can charge for their services. This means that the community suffers unnecessary shortages of professionals.

They do a bad job. Doctors' drug prescriptions cause bad side-effects and sometimes dependency. Their diagnostic tests do more harm than good in many cases. Women in particular suffer at their hands. Many iatrogenic diseases affect only them, for example those stemming from using contraceptive pills and devices and from hysterectomies. Doctors 'medicalise' pregnancy and birth, taking control away from women and treating them merely as 'cases' . Doctors and social workers can and do abuse their power, as occurred in the Cleveland child abuse scandal of 1987 (see the British Humanities Index for references to newspaper accounts of this). Generally the professionalisation of medicine means that responsibility for our health and our lives is taken out of our hands and put in those of doctors, nurses, psychiatrists, social workers and the rest. This alienates us from our own existence.

Examination question

> 'The medical profession exercises a monopoly power over health care and does so largely in its own interests.' Assess this view.
>
> AEB AS-level, June 1993, Paper 2, question 6

The Welfare State and inequality

Many proponents of the Welfare State argue that its aim is more than the elimination of the 'five giants' identified by Beveridge. It is also there to bring about greater equality within British society. This 'strategy of equality' (as the historian R. H. Tawney called it) involves funding services and benefits for the worse off by taxing the better off – the Robin Hood Welfare State. On the face of it this would appear to be happening: richer people 'obviously' pay more in to the Welfare State and poorer people equally obviously get more out. But do they? In order to see whether this is really the case we need to examine closely the two central propositions in the idea of the strategy of equality:

The best off contribute most money towards the Welfare State.

The worst off receive most benefits and services from it.

> *Why has the Conservatives' tax policy had the result of being less redistributive than previous tax regimes? (Look again at the arguments of the New Right, pp. 24–26 and 13–14.)*

Trying to assess the overall effect of taxation to determine whether it is progressive, regressive or proportional is quite difficult. Table 8.2 summarises the arguments. Income tax and National Insurance combined are progressive until the middle levels of income, then they are proportional. Thus the middle fifth of income earners pay as much (as a proportion of their income) as the highest two fifths, but more than the lowest two fifths.

Table 8.2 The best off contribute most money towards the Welfare State

Arguments in favour	Arguments against
Income tax is progressive – i.e. the better off have to pay a higher percentage on much of their income than the basic rate paid by the lower earners. The lower earners have a fairly high proportion of tax-free income (i.e. the tax threshold is quite high). Higher earners pay tax on a higher proportion of their income. National Insurance contributions are based on a percentage of salary so that the poor pay less as their incomes are lower. Insurance-based benefits, though, are frequently at a fixed level.	Yes, it is progressive, but far less so than in the past. The better off had to pay well over the basic rate on much of their income. The tax threshold has been falling for years relative to incomes, bringing even quite poor people into the tax net and increasing the number of taxpayers. There is an upper limit on earnings beyond which National Insurance contributions are not deducted. So, while the poorest pay NI on most of their income, the better off escape it on a substantial part of theirs. Also NI is not payable on income such as rent, interest from savings accounts and dividends from shares.
VAT is paid at 17.5 per cent on goods; but many basic necessities are VAT free, which helps the poor, who spend much of their income on these things. Council Tax is progressive too because it is based on the estimated value of a person's house (arranged in bands of value) and because certain classes of people are exempt.	Different rates of VAT (higher on luxury goods) have been abolished and VAT has been levied on an increasingly wide range of products. The poorest pay more VAT as a proportion of income because they spend most of their income on goods while the rich can save much of theirs. Direct taxes like VAT are regressive – they hit the poorest hardest. Council Tax is more regressive than its predecessor, council rates. A large family living in a small house will pay more than a single person or couple in a large, expensive one.
Capital is taxed as well as income (e.g. by Capital Transfer Tax) and this form is likely to be paid only by the better off.	True, but less than 2 per cent of government income is derived from this source, compared to about 25 per cent from income tax and 12.5 per cent from VAT. The non payment of capital tax by the poor is outweighed by their greater payment of excise duty on alcohol and tobacco, both in real terms and as a proportion of their income.

Commodity taxes such as VAT and excise duty are very regressive, as was the Poll Tax. Capital taxes, on the other hand, are progressive. Overall the evidence indicates that while the very poorest pay less tax than everybody else, those above the very lowest levels of income will pay the same amount of tax as a proportion of income, regardless of the level of their income. So the Robin Hood state takes from the rich, the comfortable and the 'nearly poor' to the same degree. But does the money go to the 'really poor'? Table 8.3 summarises the arguments on this issue.

The evidence shows that overall the welfare benefit system certainly helps to reduce poverty considerably, but it does not seem to do much to bring about greater equality. Julian LeGrand (1985) argues:

> 'of all current expenditure on social services it can be estimated that only about one fifth is directed primarily at the poor. All the rest is either distributed equally or towards the better off.'

Table 8.3 The worst off receive most benefits and services from the Welfare State.

Arguments in favour	Arguments against
The poor benefit most from means-tested benefits such as income support because only they are eligible for them.	Yes, but in terms of government spending most money goes on universal benefits – i.e. ones received by everybody in a certain category regardless of income. These include pensions, child benefit, invalidity benefit, unemployment and sickness benefit. Also the better off will gain more from the 'fiscal social security' of tax relief on private pensions following the 1986 Social Security Act as they will be most likely to take out such pension plans.
The poor benefit most from state health and education services because the better off can opt out into the private system.	Yes, but many people never go private, and those who do still take advantage of many state services. Furthermore, the better off are more likely to send their children to higher education (which is subsidised by the state) and the state schools their children do attend are likely to be better funded and more successful than those in deprived areas.
The poor are the only ones likely to take advantage of council housing, so they benefit from its subsidies.	Yes, but council housing now has to pay its own way and better off tenants are buying their council houses, leaving only low-quality housing for those who remain. Home owners get tax relief on mortgages regardless of their income (more 'fiscal social security').
The poor are sicker than the better off (see p. 74), therefore they will make most use of the health services. Inhabitants of inner-city areas have good access to excellent hospitals.	They do, but the better off generally have greater access to better facilities of all sorts and make proportionately greater use of them relative to their level of health.
The poor make greater use of public transport and so benefit from state subsidy of it.	Actually the better off benefit most from transport subsidies – especially rail (e.g. the London commuters) and from road building and maintenance programmes. The better off get hidden subsidies in the form of company cars, expense accounts, company pensions, membership of private health schemes and other perks. This 'occupational welfare' is subsidised by the state through tax relief to companies that provide it.

Table 8.4 The effects of taxes and benefits on inequality 1982 (% share of total income)

Group	Original income	Gross income	Disposable income	Final income
Top fifth	47	41	40	39
Next fifth	27	25	24	24
Middle fifth	18	18	18	18
Next fifth	7	11	12	12
Bottom fifth	0.4	5.7	6.8	6.9

Source: LeGrand (1985)

Original income = before taxes or state subsidies

Gross income = original income plus income subsides such as income support

Disposable income = gross income less income tax

Final income = disposable income plus the value of all subsidies like public transport less the cost of commodity taxes like VAT

Table 8.4 demonstrates the effect of taxes and benefits on inequality.

1 What were the shares of original income of the top and bottom 40 per cent of the population in 1982?

2 What was the effect of taxes and benefits on inequality in 1982?

3a Students should divide into two groups.

● *One is led by the Minister of Health in a radical new government that wishes to see fundamental changes in the medical profession. Senior civil servants are on hand to help him/her formulate the proposals. Before the meeting the members should do some research on the present problems with the medical profession to determine precisely what needs to be put right. Refer to Illich (1975) and Graham and Oakley (1981).*

● *The second group represent the BMA. They should develop all the arguments and evidence they can to try to persuade the minister and his/her advisers that change would be a bad thing. Try to predict the arguments that will be raised in the meeting and prepare counters to them, as well as being ready to put your own side of the case. Decide what threats you can make if the minister is intransigent.*

3b When both sides are ready, hold the meeting. The minister, advised by the civil servants, must make a decision at the end of it. S/he should try to be as open-minded as possible and make a realistic assessment of the possible consequences of any decision.

Public versus private medicine

In 1979, 2.8 million people were covered by private medical insurance. By 1988 the figure was 5.7 million (10 per cent of the population). The biggest single increase happened in 1980 with a 26 per cent rise. The market is dominated by the big three: the British United Provident Association (BUPA), Private Patients Plan (PPP) and Western Provident Association (WPA). BUPA has 60 per cent of the market. Table 8.5 debates the relative merits of public and private medicine.

1 Some of the points in the left and right columns of Table 8.5 can be said to answer each other. Rearrange the columns to match the points that address the same issues.

Table 8.5 The pros and cons of private medicine

Cons	Pros
Private patients see the same consultants as NHS ones – they do not get improved treatment.	There are shorter waiting lists in private practice, so patients can get treatment quickly.
Private hospitals have a limited range of facilities and full-time staff compared to NHS hospitals.	Consultants treat private patients better (e.g. they are more likely to be on time for appointments).
Private hospitals find it difficult to recruit full-time doctors because they have not been accredited for training purposes. High-quality staff, in particular, are difficult to attract.	Private patients in hospital get privacy and one-to-one treatment.
Staff are expensively trained by the NHS and then lost to the private sector, which is a drain on state resources.	Medical and paramedical staff can increase their earnings through private practice.
Some consultants may artificially create NHS waiting lists in order to attract more patients into private practice.	The NHS benefits from income from pay beds, donations of equipment by private medicine to be used for NHS and private patients, and reduced waiting lists resulting from patients going private rather than joining NHS lists.
If doctors spend time on private patients they have less time for NHS ones, thus lengthening NHS waiting times.	
NHS staff have an additional workload as a result of doctors being absent on private medical business.	Some consultants invest in private hospitals and benefit from the income they generate.
Pay beds – rented out to the private sector by the NHS – often cost more to service than the money they raise, especially when private patients in them require treatment which is heavily capital or labour intensive.	There are increasing numbers of private facilities for geriatric and other chronic medical cases.
	Some sorts of treatment are only available under private medicine – e.g. cosmetic surgery.
Private medicine can lead to 'medical inflation', i.e. doctors provide unnecessary treatment for profit.	Private medicine gives the individual choice – it is patient-centred, not run on bureaucratic lines.
Medical resources are even more concentrated in the affluent parts of the country because private medicine is attracted there.	Competition between private companies improves the service all round.
Administrative costs are higher because of the complicated and replicated fee and payment structure and advertising costs.	Some private hospitals do train nurses.
	Private medicine generates profit and attracts foreigners to this country for paid treatment, thus adding to the national wealth.
Private medicine in general is good at 'cure' not 'care' (i.e. acute rather than chronic medicine).	
There are ethical problems if doctors are shareholders in private hospitals.	Private pharmaceutical companies generate new drugs and techniques very successfully; private medical care organisations can be similarly innovative.
Generally, the state should take responsibility for the health of its people, cheque-book medicine only increases social divides.	

the same issues.

2 *What ethical problems might result from a doctor being a shareholder in a private hospital?*

There are basically three types of private medicine:

• fee for service

• private insurance cover

• premiums to medical organisations.

Agencies providing private medicine range from charitable organisations (for example church-run hospitals) to provident organisations (e.g. BUPA, which is theoretically non-profit making but in fact has subsidiaries that are profit-oriented) to 'for profit' organisations such as American Medical International.

Devise a questionnaire designed to elicit people's attitudes to private medicine. If possible, conduct the survey.

Examination question

'Health care is more effectively provided by the private sector than by the public sector.' Evaluate the sociological arguments for and against this view.

BUPA advertises the benefits of its private medicine schemes.

AEB A-level, Winter 1994, Paper 2, question 5

Drugs and society

Before beginning this section, complete the following sentences individually. Then compare and discuss what you have written with other group members:

When thinking about drugs I think about . . .

Drug users tend to be . . .

The media's portrayal of drug use is . . .

People use drugs because . . .

The effects of drugs are . . .

The drug we need to worry most about is . . .

We can find drug users easily if we go to . . .

Common conceptions about drugs

Drug users have particular characteristics. For example, the typical heroin user, as identified by studies of those who come to the attention of doctors, police or the social services, is likely to fit the following description:

– male

– in his late teens or early twenties (the average age is dropping)

– single

– the product of a single-parent family or separated from both parents

– poorly educated

– unemployed or in casual labour

– unable to give up the drug

– suffering from illnesses associated with drug use

– with a criminal record unrelated to drug use

– on prescribed drugs to control and limit his use of heroin.

Why might this be an inaccurate description of the average heroin user?

Solvent abusers ('glue sniffers'), on the other hand, tend to be:

– between 11 and 16 years old

– male

– short-term users

– concentrated in one locality.

Cocaine users are likely to be older and more affluent than either of these.

Particular areas of the country have a drug problem. For example, Liverpool has become known as 'Smack City' in the tabloids, and Merseyside in general is viewed as having a drugs problem.

'Soft' drug use leads on to 'hard' drugs. The addict is likely to climb a drugs ladder which looks like this:

Opiates, including heroin (smack, junk)

LSD (acid)

Mixed drugs (e.g. ecstasy = amphetamines + LSD)

Barbiturates (sleepers, downers)

Amphetamines (pep-pills, speed, uppers)

Cannabis (grass, pot, hash)

Hallucinogenic (magic) mushrooms

Solvents ('glue sniffing')

Figure 8.16 In general, society regards alcohol and tobacco as 'good drugs'.

Once on this ladder of bad drugs the user becomes progressively 'hooked' – physically addicted to the effects of the drug. Coming off them will require a very unpleasant and prolonged period of adjustment involving severe physical symptoms.

Climbing the ladder is expensive. Eventually the user will have to turn to crime to fund the habit. Violent crime is made more likely by the loss of inhibitions caused by drug use.

There are 'good drugs' and 'bad drugs'. 'Good' ones are fairly harmless, even beneficial. They include tobacco, caffeine and medically prescribed drugs such as Librium and Valium. Alcohol is also a 'good drug' (or it is not even thought of as a drug at all), though it is potentially harmful if taken by the wrong kind of people.

What is needed is strong will-power, to resist drugs in the first place and get off the ladder as soon as possible. The user needs to 'Just say no' (the catchphrase of a campaign against drug use launched by Nancy Reagan during her husband's US presidency). Individual free will, not economic or social circumstances, is to blame. There are strong connections here with the 'culture of poverty' theory – people can and should choose to reject that culture. This is the only way, too, to combat the spread of HIV which results from the shared use of contaminated needles for drug injection.

The reason why people become drug takers in the first place (despite the obvious drawbacks) is that they are persuaded by drug pushers who are concerned purely with profit. It is they to whom one should 'just say no'.

Generally, how do you respond to this view of drugs and drug users?

Problems with the 'commonsense' view

Users who come to the attention of the official agencies are not typical. The middle class and those who have never needed or wanted to refer themselves to agencies are under-represented in the studies and statistics.

Similarly, areas of the country with large numbers of 'drug-prone types' will be targeted in the press as problem-centres. Academic studies will then concentrate on them, giving them further prominence. In fact virtually everyone uses drugs of some sort (including alcohol, caffeine and 'medical drugs') and every society in history, with the exception of two Eskimo tribes, has had a drug or drugs as a central part of its culture. Ours is alcohol, in some Muslim countries it is hashish, in Mexico is was hallucinogens from cacti, and so on.

Evidence shows that many people experiment with drugs and never use them again. Even persistent drug users go through periods of heavy and light use. There is little hard evidence for a 'progression up the ladder' hypothesis. Instead there are 'experimental users' (in the majority) who experiment and stop, 'recreational users' who use one type of drug occasionally and without problems, and 'problem users' (in the minority) who are dependent and for whom, or for those around them, their drug-taking is causing a problem.

Figure 8.17 Poster advertising Death cigarettes. Many shops refused to stock the new brand. Why do you think this was?

So-called 'good' drugs can be more harmful than 'bad' drugs. Smoking nicotine causes about 100,000 premature deaths every year in the UK. Persistent heavy drinking causes brain cell and liver damage. In 1986 there were 18,000 hospital admissions for alcohol-related disorders, not to mention the hundreds of thousands of alcohol-related crimes. 'Medical' drugs such as the benzodiazapines Librium, Valium and Mogadon (commonly known as tranquillisers and/or sleeping pills) cause physical and psychological dependence and symptoms such as depression, tiredness, difficulty in concentration, agoraphobia and headaches. About half a million people have suffered at least a mild dependence on them and around 3.5 million people have taken tranquillisers 'well into the period when they may have lost their useful effect, and become potentially dangerous', according to one survey. Most of those prescribed benzodiazapines are women (four to each man).

One expert (Robertson 1987) states that 'bad' drugs such as heroin, cocaine and cannabis produce no such tissue damage, and problems arising from their use stem mainly from their illegal status and subsequent impurity, contamination and septic use. Another author (Young 1971) uses the term 'Law of Inverse Effect' to describe the relationship between our attitudes to a drug and the damage it does.

Expecting users to exercise total abstinence is unrealistic. Instead they should be offered free needles and syringes to help combat the spread of HIV and perhaps even be provided with injectable drugs such as heroin, or at least 'replacements' like oral methadone. This would undercut the trade in drugs like heroin and therefore also combat the spread of HIV.

1 *Brainstorm the following questions in small groups:*

Why is so much negative attention paid by the media and the government to the drugs which damage the smallest number of people, while so little is paid to the most damaging ones – alcohol and tobacco?

Why are drugs like cannabis, etc., illegal when they do so little damage, yet tobacco and alcohol are legal and freely available (with only loosely enforced rules regarding age limits)?

2 *In larger groups, collate and discuss your ideas*

Educationalists and those in positions of responsibility are very concerned about the use of 'bad' drugs by the young, but a *New Society* survey conducted in 1986 showed that the young are far more likely to use the 'good' drugs, as Table 8.6 shows.

Table 8.6 Drug use by age and sex

	Total	Male	Female	Under 14	14–16	17–19	Over 19
Total in sample	2,417	725	1,692	235	977	992	213
Which of the following have you tried? (Figures are given in percentages.)							
Cigarettes	65	64	65	60	67	63	69
Cannabis	17	24	14	7	12	19	37
Heroin	2	3	1	3	1	1	5
Solvents	6	10	4	8	6	6	6
Alcohol	89	90	88	85	88	92	82
Not stated	7	6	8	10	8	6	10
Which of the following drugs do you think is the most dangerous in terms of the effect it has? (Figures in percentages.)							
Cigarettes	21	22	20	14	20	22	25
Cannabis	2	2	1	3	1	2	1
Heroin	56	55	57	71	61	52	40
Solvents	5	4	5	3	5	5	3
Alcohol	16	16	16	8	12	18	29
Not stated	1	1	1	1	1	1	2

Source: Williams (1986)

1 *What conclusions can be drawn from the results outlined in Table 8.6?*

Why should these conclusions be treated cautiously?

2 *In the light of the above information, come up with ideas for a government health warning poster, like the one in Figure 8.18 but for cigarettes and/or whisky.*

Figure 8.18 Aiming to change people's behaviour: the DSS tries to limit drug use.

Evidence now points to the fact that 'addiction' is the wrong word to use as it implies physical need for a substance. Specialists in the field now prefer to use the word *dependence*. This means a psychological and/or physical compulsion to take a drug in order to experience its effects or to avoid the discomfort of its absence. Alcohol and the opiates (e.g. opium, morphine, methadone) create both physical and psychological compulsions. Current research suggests that amphetamines, cocaine, cannabis and the hallucinogens (such as LSD) create a psychological compulsion only (though this is not certain).

Users of proscribed drugs are by definition 'criminals'. Some drug users will in any case be criminals just as some tobacco smokers are – their criminality is unrelated to their drug use. Furthermore, if we assume that drug users are more likely to come from the poorer section of the community (though this is not necessarily the case, as we saw above), we would expect them to have a higher rate of recorded crime anyway as this section of society is more criminal (at least according to official statistics) than the rest. The question is, does drug use result in a subsequently greater chance of criminal activity in the individual than would otherwise be the case? The answer is that we do not really know, and even if we did the reasons would not be clear. They could be the need for money and decreased inhibitions or be more complex than this. Young (1971) argues that the police's pursuit of drug-takers marginalises them from ordinary society, forcing them into a closed world and turning them into criminals by making life difficult for them in the 'straight' world. This process illustrates well the point that the interactionist Howard Becker (1963) was making when he wrote:

> 'Social groups create deviance by making the rules whose infraction constitutes deviance.'

In other words, if (in this case) proscribed drugs were legalised there would be no greater crime associated with them than with tobacco or alcohol.

Many experts in the field see drug taking not as a sign of individual weakness in not being able to 'just say no' but as a product of particular social and economic circumstances. Like alcohol, drugs such as opium and methadone give a sense of well-being and release from current problems. The fit person with good prospects may not need this but the person who was a failure at school, has limited prospects and lives in a deprived area will find drugs a convenient escape route. This view of drug use and users accords more with the poverty trap approach of the Social Democrats than the culture of poverty thesis of the New Right.

Young (1971) argues that pushers are the product of the law enforcement activities of the police which have restricted the supply of drugs and hence pushed their price up. Seeing a highly profitable market develop, the criminal world moved into the drugs trade, and the pusher arrived. In the case of heroin Robertson (1987) argues:

'Most [dealers of heroin] are users themselves and finance their own use this way rather than indulging in other criminal activities . . . The stereotype of pushers who hang around street corners or outside schools and tempt newcomers to use drugs is equally fallacious and likely, if it did occur, to increase the chances of being arrested rather than increase profits.'

A meeting has been called by the Director of a college in your area to discuss the issue of drug abuse by young people at the college and in the area generally. It must do the following:

- *Write a policy statement for the college – i.e. a statement of the 'position' of the college on drugs. It may be adopted by the County Council as a whole.*

- *Incorporate in it a set of guidelines for staff employed by the Council on how to deal with any drug abuse that comes to their attention (e.g among students at the college).*

The meeting is chaired by the Director and it comprises:

Local business people (from the college's governing body)
The community policeman/woman
Social and youth workers employed by the County
Lecturers at the college
A specialist running a hostel for drug abusers trying to come off them
A doctor
An education adviser from County Hall
The lecturer in charge of running the pastoral care system in the college
Parents (from the college's governing body).

1 *Choose your roles and spend about 10 minutes working out your position on the issue in detail (make notes if you need to). At the end of that time the meeting should be convened by the Director. From then on, act in role. It is the Director's responsibility, as chair, to ensure that the aims of the meeting are achieved within the time allocated.*

2 *The three columns in Table 8.7 list types of drug, effects and long-term risk. However, they have been jumbled up! Your task is to match the entries in the three columns with each other. Then you should say whether each type of drug is: legal, illegal, illegal to sell to anyone under a certain age, illegal for someone under a certain age to buy or use, legal unless made into a preparation, illegal unless prescribed, or legal but only available on prescription.*

Answers are in the bibliography

Table 8.7 Drugs and their effects

Drug	Effects and manner of use	Risk
1. SOLVENTS (e.g. glue, lighter fuel)	1 It makes you feel happy and sociable. It can give an energy lift. Its effect can last some hours. It is taken in tablet form.	1 There appears to be limited risk as the number of users is thought to be very large and reported cases of illness and death few in number. However, there have been some deaths, possibly due to contamination of the drug.
2. AMPHETAMINES ('speed', 'uppers')	2 It makes you feel warm and drowsy, kills pain. It can cause constipation and a feeling of sickness. Under its influence it is difficult to concentrate and your reactions are slowed. It can be smoked, sniffed or injected and its effects can last for several hours.	2 Users need to take larger and larger doses to get the same effect. There is a risk of paranoia which can develop into serious mental illness. Neglect of the dietary and sleep needs of the body under the influence of the drug can lead to illness. It is difficult to break the habit, and high doses can damage the heart.
3. LSD ('acid')		
4. CAFFEINE (e.g. coffee)	3 It relaxes you, increases the pulse rate and the blood pressure while reducing the appetite. It produced carbon monoxide which is absorbed by the lungs. Its effect can last for some hours. It is smoked or chewed.	
5. BARBITURATES (sleeping pills, etc)		3 People can do dangerous things while hallucinating, including accidentally killing themselves. It can also lead to mental illness. Deaths from overdose are unknown, though, and physical addiction seems not to occur.
6. TRANQUILISERS ('speed', 'uppers')	4 It is absorbed into the bloodstream. Small amounts make you friendly, relaxed and talkative, large amounts make speech blurred, vision diminished, concentration reduced and reactions slowed. Its effects can last for some hours. It is swallowed.	
7. CANNABIS ('grass', 'pot', etc.)		4 The main risk is from accidental death or injury while affected, choking on vomit following unconsciousness, and freezing the tubes in the lungs as a result of squirting the very cold gas into the mouth. It can result in brain damage in the long term.
8. MAGIC MUSHROOMS	5 It makes you feel strong and confident, reduces the appetite and enables you to work harder. However, you feel tired and depressed after it has worn off (which is not very long after taking it). It is sniffed up the nose or injected in to the bloodstream.	
9. COCAINE ('coke', 'snow', etc.)		5 This can cause damage to the heart, liver, stomach and brain. Accidents and violence resulting from the diminished control over one's actions is the major cause of the many deaths and injuries related to this drug. Overdose or choking on vomit following unconsciousness are also risks. Occasional heavy use can result in headaches, sickness and irritability, headaches and depression.
10. HEROIN-like drugs ('smack', 'H', etc.)		
11. TOBACCO	6 It affects people in different ways, and some claim not to be affected by it. Small amounts can result in a feeling of well-being, talkativeness and giggling, larger amounts in forgetfulness and withdrawal. These effects usually subside after an hour or so. It is usually smoked (mixed with tobacco) or eaten.	
12. ALCOHOL		6 An overdose can be fatal, and there is a risk of infection from AIDS and other diseases through needle sharing. People become dependent quickly and withdrawal is painful, leading to shakes, sweating, stomach cramps and so on. Addiction to the drug can lead to dangerous activities to obtain it.
13. ECSTASY	7 You may become light-headed, feel very confident and even see and hear things with greater clarity. Hallucinations are possible, and you may feel sick and get stomach ache. Effects can last for as much as a day. It is usually drunk as a tea or eaten, sometimes cooked (e.g. in a cake).	

Drug	Effects and manner of use	Risk
	8 You feel relaxed and will go to sleep with larger doses (and this drug is often used for this). (After taking several of these the user loses control of speech and other faculties. The effect can last for up to six hours and the drug is usually taken in pill form (though it can be injected as a diluted powder).	7 Deaths are rare though if it is injected there is a risk of infection from shared needles. There seems to be a high risk of physical dependence, though if it is given up there are a few long-term consequences.
	9 It calms you down and makes you feel drowsy. It makes you feel less anxious and stressed, and is often used specifically for this. It lasts for up to six hours and is usually taken in pill form (though it can be injected as a diluted powder).	8 There are a few serious consequences, though some people suffer a deterioration in memory and some may become temporarily mentally disturbed. There can be a risk of lung damage when smoked and it is dangerous to drive under its influence.
	10 It keeps you awake and aids concentration. A lot can increase the heart rate and make you shaky as well as increasing the number of times you urinate. Its effects can last for a number of hours and it is usually drunk.	9 The biggest risk is in picking the wrong sort as come varieties are poisonous. There are no withdrawal symptoms and apparently no long-term damage, though high doses can cause temporary sickness and stomach pain.
	11 It makes you energetic and alert, though it can increase anxiety levels. One dose can last for two days and when it has worn off you very often feel tired, depressed and hungry. It is usually taken as tablets, though can be injected or sniffed.	10 Accidents can result from loss of body control. Large doses can cause loss of consciousness, breathing problems and death (this drug is sometimes used as a method of suicide). Mixing with alcohol can be very dangerous.
	12 It can have quite powerful effects on your senses and perceptions, perhaps causing hallucinations. While under its influence you are unable to do much, and might be very excited or – if you have a 'bad trip' – terrified.	11 Peptic ulcers, cancer and heart disease are thought to be made more likely by the use of this drug in large quantities (say, more than 8 cups a day). Physical dependence can occur, and withdrawal leads to headaches, irritability and drowsiness.
	13 It goes directly to the brain and makes you feel light-headed. Its effect is quite short lived (usually less than an hour) and may leave you with a hangover (though it can also be fatal). It is always sniffed through the nose, sometimes from inside a plastic bag over the head.	12 People using this drug need more and more to get the same effect and eventually feel that they cannot live normally without it. Withdrawal can cause anxiety, sickness and headaches, even fits (after high doses).
		13 Regular use can result in cancer, blood clots, heart disease, strokes, poor circulation and ulcers. Withdrawal from regular use can result in irritability, headaches and depression.

Bibliography

Abbott, P. and Payne, G. (1990) *New Directions in the Sociology of Health,* Lewes: Falmer

Baggott, R. (1994) *Health and Health Care in Britain,* New York: St Martin's Press

Barry, G. *et al.* (eds) (1965) *Health and Wealth,* London: Macdonald

Becker, H. (1963) *Outsiders: Studies in the Sociology of Deviance,* New York: Free Press

Breckon, W. (1978) *Your Everyday Drugs,* London: BBC

Clover, A. (1984) *Homeopathy: A Patient's Guide,* Wellingborough: Thorsons

DHSS (1985) *The Reform of Social Security,* Vol. 2, Cmnd 9518, London: HMSO

Dingwall, R. and Lewis, P. (eds) (1983) *The Sociology of the Professions: Lawyers, Doctors and Others,* London: Macmillan

Glennerster, H. (ed.) (1983) *The Future of the Welfare State,* London: Heinemann (see especially article by LeGrand)

Goode, W. J. (1978) *The Celebration of Heroes: Prestige as a Social Control System,* Berkeley, CA: University of California Press

Goffman, E. (1984) *Asylums,* Harmondsworth: Penguin

Graham, H. (1985) *Health and Welfare,* London: Macmillan

—— and Oakley, A. (1981) 'Ideologies of reproduction', in H. Roberts (ed.) *Women, Health and Reproduction,* London: Routledge

Grills, J. and Grills, M. (1986) *Drug Abuse,* Oxford: Oxford University Press

Hart, G. (1990) 'Say no to drugs, but yes to clean syringes?', 1in Abbott and Payne (1990)

Higgins, J. (1988) *The Business of Medicine: Private Health Care in Britain,* London: Macmillan

Illich, I. (1975) *Medical Nemesis,* London: Marion Boyars

Inglis, B. (1979) *Natural Medicine,* London: Collins (contains a useful list of addresses of organisations)

Lacey, R. and Woodward, S. (1985) *That's Life! Survey on Tranquillisers,* London: BBC

LeGrand, J. (1982) *The Strategy of Equality,* London: Allen & Unwin

—— (1985) *Open University Course D210,* block 5, units 18 and 19, Milton Keynes: Open University Press

Mann, F. (1973) *Acupuncture: Cure of Many Diseases,* London: Pan

Mathews, R. (1979) 'Decarceration and the fiscal crisis', in B. Fine *et al.* (eds) *Capitalism and the Rule of Law,* London: Hutchinson

Observer Modern Studies Handbook: Drugs, London: Observer, 1986

Pinchuck, T. and Clark, R. (1984) *Medicine for Beginners,* London: Writers and Readers

Robertson, R. (1987) *Heroin, AIDS and Society,* London: Hodder & Stoughton

Robinson, R. (1990) *Competition and Health Care,* London: King's Fund Institute

Salmon, J. W. (1984) *Alternative Medicines: Popular and Policy Perspectives,* London: Tavistock

Scull, A. (1984) *Decarceration: Community Treatment and the Deviant, a Radical View,* London: Polity

Stanway, A. (1986) *Alternative Medicine: A Guide to Natural Therapies,* 2nd edn, Harmondsworth: Penguin (has a good bibliography)

The Times, 14 August 1985 (carried a useful report on trials of alternative therapies)

Thomson, D. (1986) 'The overpaid elderly?', *New Society,* 7 March

Tinker, A. (1984) *The Elderly in Modern Britain,* 2nd edn, London: Longman

Trowler, P. (1987) *Active Sociology,* London: HarperCollins

Weitz, M. (1980) *Health Shock,* Newton Abbot: David & Charles

Wells, N. and Freer, C. (eds) (1988) *The Ageing Population: Burden or Challenge?,* London: Macmillan

Williams, M. (1986) 'The Thatcher generation', *New Society,* 21 February

Young, J. (1971) 'The role of the police as amplifiers of deviancy', in S. Cohen (ed.) *Images of Deviance,* Harmondsworth: Penguin

Useful addresses

Age Concern
Astral House
1268 London Rd
London SW16 4ER
Teel: 0181 679 8000

ASH
109 Gloucester Place
London W1
Tel: 0171 935 3519

Others include gender, ethnicity and age, for example. Making these kinds of points means that you are not **just** restating in another way what you said earlier.

4. Chapter 6, p. 100.

'Women's health chances, the health care they receive and their responsibility for the health care of others – all these can only be understood in the context of their gender roles in a patriarchal society'. Explain and discuss this view.

(AEB AS level, Summer 1994, paper 2, question 6)

Good	Bad
Intro: Goes into detail on the question: defines and explains 'health chances', 'gender roles' and 'patriarchal society'. Suggests that different feminist (and other) approaches will tend to stress one explanation more than the other (eg liberal feminists emphasise the patriarchal nature of society). Points out that there are three parts to the question which will be dealt with separately – this leads in to a map of the essay structure.	*Intro*: Goes straight into a discussion of, for example, Graham and Oakley. Does not address the question or map the answer.
Body: Divides this into three. 1. Health chances: gives evidence on morbidity and mortality by gender, showing current patterns and historical trends. Critically reviews explanations of them (referring back to the 'gender roles' and 'patriarchal society' issues regularly). Suggests other factors than gender roles and patriarchal society which influence women's health chances. 2. Health care: discusses, eg, the critique of the patriarchal nature of pregnancy and childbirth provided by Graham and Oakley and relates this to male and female gender roles and the particular patriarchal characteristics of society they consider important. Addresses these ideas critically. 3. Health care of others: Reviews the role of the women within the health services and in the community, including the responsibilities they tend to have for ageing or sick relatives outside the formal (statutory, voluntary or private) health care provision. Again relates the discussion to gender roles and the idea of a patriarchal society. Suggests other factors than gender roles and patriarchal society which influence women's role in the health care of others.	*Body*: Uses this essay as an oppportunity to complain about the ill-treatment women receive or some other aspect of inequality, without attempting to review dispassionately all sides of the issue using different sorts of evidence (statistical, academic research) and logical argument.
Conclusion: Comes to conclusions about the three issues separately, in each case evaluating the strength of both the sex roles and patriarchal society arguments as explanations. Points out that the word 'only' in the questions make it more difficult to agree in an unqualified way with the statement. Also points out that the title specifies 'their' (women's) gender roles, ignoring men's gender roles which are implicated too.	*Conclusion:* Comes to a simplistic conclusion which relates to only part of the question.

Index

,6

British Homeopathic Association
27a Devonshire St
London W1N 1RJ
Tel: 0171 935 2163

Chiropractic Advancement Association
56 Barnes Crescent
Wimborne
Dorset
BH21 2AZ

Institute for Complementary Medicine
21 Portland Place
London W1N 3AF
Tel: 0171 636 9543

Institute for the Study of Drug Dependence
1 Hatton Place
London EC1N 8ND
Tel: 0171 928 1211
(For information on drugs, particularly a very
useful booklet called *Drug Abuse Briefing*)

National Council on Alcoholism
3 Grosvenor Crescent
London SW1 7EL
Q Directory
17 Wolseley Rd
London N8

Society for the Study of Holistic Health
160 Upper Fant Road
Maidstone
Kent
ME16 8DJ

Vegan Society
47 Highlands Rd
Leatherhead
Surrey

Answers to activity

The answers to the Drugwise exercise pp. 143–4
are as follows (each set of three numbers refers to
columns 1, 2 and 3 respectively):

1, 13, 4 (legal)

2, 11, 2 (illegal unless prescribed)

3, 12, 3 (illegal)

4, 10, 11 (legal)

5, 8, 10 (illegal unless prescribed)

6, 9, 12 (legal but only available on prescription)

7, 6, 8 (illegal)

8, 7, 9 (legal unless made into a preparation)

9, 5, 7 (illegal)

10, 2, 6 (illegal unless prescribed)

11, 3, 13 (illegal to sell to anyone under 16)

12, 4, 5 (legal to buy over 18 and to use at any
age over 5 away from licensed premises)

13, 1, 1 (illegal)

Appendix: Skeleton answers

1. Chapter 1, p. 4

'Health and illness must be seen as conditions which are both socially caused and socially defined'. Examine the evidence for this view.

(AEB AS level, Summer 94, paper 2, question 5)

Good	Bad
Intro: Discusses the possible meanings of 'socially caused' and 'socially defined'. Socially defined could mean, for example, micro-social situations (eg in the family or in a sub-cultural group) or macro-social ones (society at large). Gives an initial discussion of the difficulties of identifying exactly what 'health' means and the difficulties of drawing the line between that and 'illness'. Maps the rest of the essay.	*Intro*: Ignores question and does not distinguish between health and illness nor between cause and definition. Doesn't problematise the word 'socially'. Begins immediately with a review of one memorised study which is relevant to only part of the question (eg Laing on schizophrenia). Makes no attempt to help the reader or indicate that the answer has been well thought-out because doesn't provide a 'map' of the structure of the essay.
Body: Discusses the social constructionist theory of health and illness. Uses, eg, Laing's work to show how mental illness can be socially defined. Critically addresses these ideas. Moves on to the 'caused' part of the question and reviews evidence on recurrent patterns in health and illness eg by class and gender. Reviews explanations which emphasize the social causes of these (eg structural-material/social selection/behavioural-cultural/stress). Discusses alternative explanations (physiological, genetic, artefact) and criticisms of the social constructionist viewpoint (eg Sheeran). Care is taken not only to describe these ideas but to evaluate them – which is what is implied by the word 'examine' in the title.	*Body:* Gives a description of a limited amount of evidence, including the outcome of a few studies and some statistics. However these are inadequate and only half remembered. No attempt is made to 'examine' the evidence for the view stated – only to recount it.
Conclusion: The conclusion treats the 'definition' and 'cause' aspects of the question separately. Comes to a conclusion about how compelling the evidence discussed earlier on is on each. Probably suggests that talking in general terms about 'health' and 'illness' is simplistic. The statement is true in some senses for some aspects of health and illness, both in terms of their definition and their cause, but we should take care not to generalise beyond this limited conclusion as the statement in the examination question does.	*Conclusion:* Comes to a simplistic conclusion. Probably agrees with the statement in the question without reservation, possibly in the mistaken belief that because the statement appears in an examination question it must be a) unproblematic and b) right.

2. Chapter 4, p. 67

'The Welfare State has blunted the extremes of poverty, but has failed to achieve its goal of eliminating it.' Explain and assess this view.

(AEB A level, June 1993, paper 2, question 7)

Good	Bad
Intro: Defines and explains the concept of the Welfare State, giving a brief historical overview of its development. Quickly describes the different parts of it which are relevant to the poverty issue. Shows that 'poverty' is a contested concept and quickly reviews different ways of defining it. Points out that how one defines poverty crucially affects the conclusions one comes to in answering this question, particularly because the word 'extremes' is interpreted in different ways when using different definitions. Notes, too, that 'blunted' is not a very precise word, which makes it difficult to assess the claim (which is what we are asked to do). Maps the rest of the essay.	*Intro:* Goes straight into a fairly simplistic account of 'definitions of poverty' but does not relate them to the question set.
Body: Discusses the ways in which the various parts of the Welfare State have tackled poverty, including recent changes, and reviews the evidence (official statistics and from studies over the years) which examine their effectiveness in this. Examines in detail the evidence about poverty today and refers back to the definition issue. Points out that the question suggests that the Welfare State has the aim of eliminating poverty ('its goal'). Notes that the personification of 'the Welfare State' implicit in the idea of it having goals is a mistake and instead paints a picture of the Welfare State as contested terrain with numerous policy makers, professionals and other 'stake-holders' having ideas about and influence on goals. Also notes that **publicly stated** policy and the reasons for it (for example as suggested by the Beveridge Report) may be different from private intentions of policy makers and possibly relates this to Merton's ideas about latent and manifest functions. Reviews the work of (eg) Gans on the functions of poverty and of LeGrand on the Welfare State never being designed to reduce inequalities in society in any fundamental way. Explains the New Right view of the Welfare State, the reasons for poverty in society and the need for the existence of poverty as a motivation for hard work. Uses these ideas to show that there are alternative perspectives on policy-makers' goals for the Welfare State.	*Body:* Describes the Welfare State but probably concentrates on its historical background rather than the situation today. Mis-spells Beveridge. Makes a rather ill-informed attempt to give evidence about changes to poverty in Britain and the role of the Welfare State in influencing these. The different parts of the Welfare State are never really described, the concept being used at too high a level of generality to be able to answer the question well.
Conclusion: Comes to an assessment of the statement in the title, particularly making a judgement about whether the **extremes** of poverty have been **blunted** by referring back to the data given in the body of the essay. Other causes than the operation of the Welfare State for changes in the extent of poverty could be suggested (eg you could argue that the extremes **have** been blunted that this has been due to economic development, not – or only partly – due to the	*Conclusion:* Accepts that it is 'the goal' of the Welfare State to eliminate poverty. Probably concludes that the Welfare State has blunted the extremes of poverty, forgetting to apply the different concepts of poverty to the idea.

Welfare State). Suggests that it was never clear that 'elimination' of poverty was the goal set for the Welfare State. Also suggests that, if this was its primary goal, it is impossible to achieve it using some definitions of poverty.

3. Chapter 5, p. 87.

Critically examine the relationship between social class background and the nature and distribution of different types of illness.

(AEB A level, Summer 1994, paper 2, question 5)

Good	*Bad*
Intro: Begins by reviewing different definitions of 'social class' showing that it is a problematic concept. Suggests that the Registrar General's definition will be used in the essay (because this is the one used for official health statistics) but notes its limitations.	*Intro*: Goes straight into a half-remembered account of the way in which the distribution of ill-health correlates with social class background. Does not problematise the concept of social class or map the essay.
Problematises the notion of 'illness' – explaining the related ideas that the definition of illness is socially constructed and that the data we have about it usually results from social processes as well as physiological and psychological 'realities'. Maps the rest of the essay, noting that 'relationship' here can mean both causal relationship and statistical relationship and that both will be explored.	
Body: Gives evidence on the way in which rates of different types of illness vary as we look across the social class scale, pointing out that most types of illness apparently increase in incidence among the more deprived social groups according to the evidence we have. Points out too that different types of illness have different geographical distributions across the country and this appears to be linked to relative levels of deprivation (and hence social class) in those areas. Reviews the historical trends on this issue. Reiterates the fact that we must treat official statistics on illness, like other types, with caution.	*Body*: Continues the social class background/illness discussion but is limited to description rather than a critical examination (as required by the question). Reviews some explanations of the link, but this is done only partially.
Moves on to discuss the different causal explanations for the evidence given above, including the structural-material, social selection, behavioural-cultural and stress explanations. Also reviews the artefact and genetic explanations, which minimise or discount the importance of social class background. Critically evaluates each of these.	
Conclusion: A difficult question to write a good conclusion to because it is so straightforward. One way to do it would be to make some summarising/generalising statements about the discussion in the body of the essay which sums it up in a few words. Finish, however, by picking up the issue about 'different types' of illness in the question, pointing out that the influence of the social class background will be greater in some than in others, with examples. You should make the important point too that social class is just one of a number of social factors which are related to issues of health and illness.	*Conclusion*: Restates earlier points and ignores the question's emphasis on *different types* of illness.

Others include gender, ethnicity and age, for example. Making these kinds of points means that you are not **just** restating in another way what you said earlier.

4. Chapter 6, p. 100.

'Women's health chances, the health care they receive and their responsibility for the health care of others – all these can only be understood in the context of their gender roles in a patriarchal society'. Explain and discuss this view.

(AEB AS level, Summer 1994, paper 2, question 6)

Good	Bad
Intro: Goes into detail on the question: defines and explains 'health chances', 'gender roles' and 'patriarchal society'. Suggests that different feminist (and other) approaches will tend to stress one explanation more than the other (eg liberal feminists emphasise the patriarchal nature of society). Points out that there are three parts to the question which will be dealt with separately – this leads in to a map of the essay structure.	*Intro*: Goes straight into a discussion of, for example, Graham and Oakley. Does not address the question or map the answer.
Body: Divides this into three. 1. Health chances: gives evidence on morbidity and mortality by gender, showing current patterns and historical trends. Critically reviews explanations of them (referring back to the 'gender roles' and 'patriarchal society' issues regularly). Suggests other factors than gender roles and patriarchal society which influence women's health chances. 2. Health care: discusses, eg, the critique of the patriarchal nature of pregnancy and childbirth provided by Graham and Oakley and relates this to male and female gender roles and the particular patriarchal characteristics of society they consider important. Addresses these ideas critically. 3. Health care of others: Reviews the role of the women within the health services and in the community, including the responsibilities they tend to have for ageing or sick relatives outside the formal (statutory, voluntary or private) health care provision. Again relates the discussion to gender roles and the idea of a patriarchal society. Suggests other factors than gender roles and patriarchal society which influence women's role in the health care of others.	*Body*: Uses this essay as an oppportunity to complain about the ill-treatment women receive or some other aspect of inequality, without attempting to review dispassionately all sides of the issue using different sorts of evidence (statistical, academic research) and logical argument.
Conclusion: Comes to conclusions about the three issues separately, in each case evaluating the strength of both the sex roles and patriarchal society arguments as explanations. Points out that the word 'only' in the questions make it more difficult to agree in an unqualified way with the statement. Also points out that the title specifies 'their' (women's) gender roles, ignoring men's gender roles which are implicated too.	*Conclusion*: Comes to a simplistic conclusion which relates to only part of the question.

Index